ORDINARY PEOPLE
Extraordinary Lives

ORDINARY PEOPLE
Extraordinary Lives

The Associate Movement in Religious Communities

Kathleen Wade, Mercy Associate

OPEL Press
Cincinnati, Ohio

All rights reserved, Published 2004
OPEL Press
2529 Concordgreen Drive
Cincinnati, OH 45244
opelpress@cinci.rr.com

ISBN 0-9755802-0-5

Library of Congress Control Number: 2004094562

Cover, Graphics and Text Design: Gertrude E. Stefanko

To

Woody
who supports me in
my writing life
my spiritual life
and my life in Mercy

Contents

Chapters

Appendix

Foreword

I was eager and naïve when I entered the Sisters of Mercy in 1959, just out of high school. I had admired the strength and dedication of the sisters who taught me in grade school, and I wanted to be like them. They led a disciplined life, but I could tell they had fun. I knew they cared about me and my family. Our Novitiate was full - over seventy adolescent girls shut off from the outside world to learn convent ways. We thought we knew what our future would be like. We envisioned an ordered life of prayer and service, as the eight-hundred other sisters in our Cincinnati Province had been living for decades.

The Second Vatican Council (Vatican II) convened in the mid-1960s, just as I was finishing college and preparing for my religious life as a teacher. Vatican II encouraged religious orders to return to the original spirit of their founders. In many cases, this called for radical change, which came too slowly for some and too quickly for others. The outward changes included a modified habit, relaxed schedule, a return to our baptismal names, freedom to drive, eat in public, and visit people in their homes. The more important changes took a lot longer and are still taking place. These include changing our understanding of women's place in church and society, working for justice in our global village, delving deeper into Scripture and theology. Meanwhile, the Catholic Church and the world continue to experience profound changes. Old paradigms no longer serve contemporary needs.

Large numbers of men and women, in response to a different call, left religious life in the years after Vatican II. The Spirit was moving in ways most didn't understand. Concurrently religious orders began welcoming women and men in different life styles to share in their prayer, ministry and community. It has taken several decades for religious to understand and accept laity as affiliates. Religious orders are grappling with temporary and alternative forms of membership. Meanwhile, lay men and women are attracted by the courage and vision of various founders. Lay people feel called to holiness and service in partnership with religious men and women, without embracing a celibate lifestyle in community.

Today few candidates enter novitiates and vowed membership is aging, but the numbers of those who want affiliate membership is growing by leaps and bounds. Our community began accepting associates in the early 1980s. I was drawn by their enthusiasm and energy. Association is pointing toward a future for religious that isn't clear. I want to be among the first of the new, whatever that is, while being one of the last of our aging members. I want to share the gift of Mercy with all people and work with them to bring compassion to our world. God knows that the needs of the world are too big for religious alone to meet, no matter how many there are. All people are called to live the Gospel and to bring about the reign of God. That's the call lay people are answering, whether they're called associates, affiliates, oblates, companions, or co-members. By whatever name, there are thousands of men and women, Catholic and otherwise, who are partnering with vowed religious on their spiritual path and working to make a difference in the world.

Several years ago Kathy Wade and I realized that this story had to be told. People are hungry for what association has to offer, but they don't know it exists. Kathy had recently retired from teaching in order to devote her time and energy to writing. We decided to take a step into the dark. We traveled around talking with associates and were deeply moved by their stories, some of which we share with you here. Our goal eluded us for a while when we couldn't find a publisher. The stories lay fallow for a period until the Spirit stirred again. Gert Stefanko, a Mercy associate of long standing and a gifted artist, offered to design the book.

This is the right moment for these stories to be shared. Many people are disillusioned by the troubles in the Catholic Church, but they don't want to give up their faith. More religious orders are welcoming associates. In faith and hope we offer these stories and pray that those who are searching will read them and be inspired to act.

Carren Herring, RSM
Co-Director, Mercy Association
Regional Community of Cincinnati

Acknowledgments

We are grateful for the support we've received from the Sisters of Mercy, especially the Regional Communities of Dallas and Cincinnati. We're grateful to all those who gave us their input: Sue Ellen Brown, Sister Mary Perpetua Overbeck, Sister Virginia Ann Froehle, Sister Patricia Schnapp, Marilyn Parks Herring, Forrest Brandt, Cheryl Endres and a group of women writers at Women Writing for (a) Change. Thanks to Elaine Schneider, Co-Director of Mercy Associates for the Cincinnati Region, for retyping parts of the manuscript when it was electronically lost. We're grateful to Vivien Schapera and Drew Logan for sharing their wisdom and experience. We thank all the associates who sent us their stories, including the many not in this book. We're grateful to those who welcomed us into their homes while we interviewed them, and the members of the Herring family who gave us hospitality during our travels. We thank NACAR and Sister Ellen O' Connell for encouragement. We trust that the God who began this work in us will see it through to completion, and that the words planted in the hearts of our readers will bear fruit in justice and mercy.

Kathleen Wade, Mercy Associate
Carren Herring, RSM

Introduction

Story is the language of faith, enabling us to express the inexpressible. It is within story that we try to verbalize the experience of our unique and intimate relationship with the God of the Universe. The Holy Spirit has recently begun to weave a new tale, that of religious associates.

Ordinary People, Extraordinary Lives is a treasury of stories told by people whose lives have been enriched through affiliation with religious women and men. Supported by the charism of various religious institutes, associates are lay women and men – and a small percentage of diocesan priests and permanent deacons – who wish to formally connect with a religious congregation for continued spiritual growth and the promotion of the institute's mission. The Associate Movement, as it has come to be known in recent years, is one of the fastest growing movements of laity within the American Catholic Church. Yet there has been little statistical data or theological reflection on it, until the North American Conference of Associates and Religious (NACAR) engaged the Center for Applied Research in the Apostolate (CARA) to conduct a groundbreaking survey in 2000 entitled, "Partners in Mission: A Profile of Associates and Religious in the United States."

Over 11,000 religious congregations across the United States received the survey's questionnaire, and seventy-five percent of those congregations responded. Across the United States, 27,400 associates were counted, with another 2,700 in formation - a revolutionary movement in the Church. (See Appendix A for details of this study.)

No matter how comprehensive statistics may be, they tell only part of the story. Behind these numbers are human faces, men and women called by God through the Holy Spirit to live out their baptismal promises in a new and radical way. The stories in this book profile men and women from across the United States who have answered the call to partner with religious communities such as the Sisters of Mercy, Maryknoll Fathers, Dominican Sisters, Sisters of St. Francis, the Incarnate Word Sisters, Passionist Fathers,

Sisters of Charity and Precious Blood Fathers. Hundreds of other religious communities have associates with similar stories.

The call to minister to the needs of the world was once reserved to "the chosen," those with vocations to the priesthood, the brotherhood, the sisterhood. The ordinary layperson did not know the sacred and sometimes secret steps within this inner circle. The phenomenon of association shows that all have been chosen to lead extraordinary lives.

The stories here manifest that no matter where we find ourselves in the workplace, we are all partners in ministry. No longer will a chosen few carry the responsibility of serving God's people. The stories of these ordinary people are eloquent testimony that the Associate Movement is here to stay.

If you find the people in this book inspiring, follow that prompting. Contact any vowed member or associate of a religious community. The web sites of those communities featured in this book are listed in the Appendix. You can also visit the web site of NACAR, a national clearinghouse, at www.catholicchurch.org/nacar.

Jean Sonnenberg, ACBS
Co-Founder, North American Conference
of Associates and Religious

One

Mary O'Connor

Associate of the Sisters of Mercy

Mary O'Connor with Sister Andre Dembowski

Judgment will be without mercy to anyone who has shown no mercy; mercy triumphs over judgment. What good is it, my brothers and sisters, if you say you have faith but do not have works? Can faith save you? If a brother or sister is naked and lacks daily food, and one of you says to them, "Go in peace; keep warm and eat your fill," and yet you do not supply their bodily needs, what is the good of that? So faith by itself, if it has no works, is dead. James 2:13-17

*C*ome *for a week or a month…* read the ad for a homeless shelter in New York City for women and children. *You might just see the face of God.* Mary O'Connor, a middle-school nurse in Wilkes-Barre, Pennsylvania, couldn't explain her attraction to that ad, but she felt it might have something to do with a recurring dream.

"When I think about it," says this wife and mother of seven, "that dream was the only way God could get my attention."

1

In the dream, she was climbing the stairs of a large house filled with women and children singing and dancing. On the top floor were a roof garden and a room especially for her.

Mary clipped the ad and stuck it on her refrigerator - next to a yellowing newspaper article about a group of sisters living in a large house in New York City. "I wasn't sure why that article seemed so important," she recalls, "but I couldn't throw it away either." The news article told how Sister Elaine Roulet, who had been working with women in prisons, had come home one night and asked the other sisters if they wouldn't mind for a few nights giving one of the extra rooms of their large convent home to a woman getting out of prison – just until she got on her feet. The sisters had agreed. Within two years, Sister Elaine had opened seven such houses for women.

Feeling some connection between the ad, the dream, and the news clipping, Mary decided to talk it over with her spiritual director, a Sister of Mercy. "I call Sister Marie my spiritual midwife," jokes Mary, her eyes dancing. "Together we've pushed, pulled and labored to give birth to Jesus over and over again in my simple little life." Sister Marie encouraged her to answer the ad, stay a week, see where it was leading her. So in mid-July, 1993, with her youngest in high school, and with the blessing of her husband, she left her comfortable suburban home.

She appeared on the doorstep of Providence House in New York City, off Flatbush Avenue. Sister Mary Doyle, a Sister of St. Joseph, greeted her and led her up three flights of steps to her room, where she saw a sunny skylight. "I had no idea where I was going," she says, "but I knew this was where I was meant to be."

During her weeklong stay, she sat around a large table with women and children – the women and children of her recurring dream. Many of the women were undocumented aliens – Dominicans, Guyanese, Jamaicans, Hispanics. Suffering from addictions or prostitution, lost and angry, they were afraid to believe there was a safe place for them and their children. "I didn't go to serve them, just to be with them," she explains. "I was the first person Loraine had ever opened up to. I would sit with her and hold her baby, and little by little she would tell me her story." During Mary's stay, this youthful grandmother did odd jobs, ran errands, cooked, and walked with the women and their kids to a nearby park.

Mary credits her "spiritual midwife," Sister Marie, with encouraging her to take the risk and step into the unknown. But Sister Marie is only one part of a wider circle connecting her to the Sisters of Mercy, going back to her high-school Latin teacher, Sister Inez Joseph. "She was barely five feet tall, but she made us feel special," Mary recalls. "She was my first role model of a formally educated woman, and she encouraged me to pursue nursing." After high school, Mary chose College Misericordia, where she lived and studied with the Sisters of Mercy for four years. "They had a profound influence on me," she says. "They instilled in us a sense of dignity and worth. They empowered us to be women of faith and vision – to see beyond but also within."

During college, Mary met John O'Connor, a student at neighboring Kings College, and in 1964 they married. Not long after, Mary set aside her nursing career for her job as full-time homemaker, while John began to establish his law practice in their small community of Wilkes-Barre. At a weekend retreat during the 1970s, Mary met Sister Andre Dembowski, and a friendship formed. "We were both struggling," Mary remembers. "I was dissatisfied with my parish's resistance to change, following the Church renewal of Vatican II." Sister Andre felt the same resistance within her religious order and was considering leaving it and joining the Sisters of Mercy.

The two friends kept in touch. Sister Andre did become a Sister of Mercy, and while she was earning her Masters in Theology, she and Mary would meet to talk. "Andre would share what she was learning, and I felt my heart on fire. She made the scriptures come alive." But Sister Andre did more than talk. She also sat in as babysitter for Mary's growing family, so that Mary could have some time for herself. "Andre taught me how important it was for me to take care of myself spiritually, to look at how God was working with my life, especially in the middle of raising a large family." It was also Sister Andre who nudged Mary toward finding a spiritual director.

In 1988, Sister Andre invited Mary and John to consider becoming Mercy Associates – a new kind of affiliation being offered by the sisters. The couple agreed to meet with others

Sister Andre had gathered together. They learned more about Catherine McAuley, the Irish socialite who unexpectedly inherited the equivalent of millions of dollars in the 1820s and used it to build the House of Mercy to educate and house poor women and children in Dublin. A few years later, yielding to pressure from Irish Bishops, Catherine established the Sisters of Mercy – an order which today ministers to thousands throughout the world. "I felt an instant attraction to Catherine," Mary remembers, "especially the way she trusted in God's Providence." Membership as an associate fit with Mary's belief that, as a layperson, she should be following her baptismal call to somehow minister to others. "Becoming a Mercy associate also fit with my longing to be more reflective, more trusting of myself."

As a Mercy associate, Mary decided to take part in a faith-sharing group within the Mercy community. "Sharing with the sisters, with single women and married couples, has been a real source of life for me," she says. "I listen to the stories of others, and I feel myself being called to a deeper level of faith, although at first, I wasn't sure what that would mean."

That is, not until the recurring dream began. Since her first visit to Providence House in New York City in 1993, she has returned each year to spend time with the homeless women and children. "It's a very holy place to be. Those living on the fringes teach me about the poor woman within me, the suffering person in me that I'd rather ignore." Until she was able to feel the neglect and poverty inside herself, she explains, "I don't think I was truly able to see that God was in these poor, these neglected women and children. I had to recognize the crucified God in myself first."

Membership in the Mercy circle of sisters and associates led her to Plymouth, Pennsylvania, and McAuley House for homeless women and their children. Mary approached Sister Lucille Brislen asking if there was something she could do. "Whenever you're cooking," Sister Lucille told her, "you could double the recipe and freeze it for us, because we never know how many we're having here." Once she began delivering her meals to McAuley House, Mary became aware of the long hours and the demands on the sisters' lives, so she decided she could stay overnight with the women once in a while to give the sisters a break.

Mary tells the story of spending an evening at the shelter just before Christmas with a woman about to have her baby. "Everything she owned was in one plastic bag," Mary recalls. As they waited for the ambulance together, the woman began telling Mary about her struggle to overcome drug addiction, and her desire to make a new life for her baby. Mary remembered the births of her own seven children – the joy and fullness of her supportive family. "Never did I have a stranger sit with me while I was waiting to give birth," she says. "That night was my Advent. At times like this you know it's not just you. I could feel the prayers of all the sisters with us. And I prayed about that lonely mother and child for a long time."

During another stay at McAuley House, Mary brewed coffee and was ready with an early morning hug and sendoff for a woman taking her sick child to a clinic. The woman questioned why Mary would go to the trouble. "I had kids, and I knew what it was like when they were sick – although I'd never had to care for them alone." Mary also had remembered how Catherine McAuley, as she was dying, requested that her sisters have a "comfortable cup of tea when I'm gone...." As a Mercy associate, Mary felt Catherine's presence, knowing she was carrying on the foundress' work.

Another evening, a resident at McAuley House returned the key to the laundry room and said to Mary, "Thank you for being here." Mary brushed it off, but the woman looked her in the eyes, repeating, "No. *Thank you for being here.* Because if you didn't stay with us, we wouldn't have any place to sleep. We'd be out on the street."

In addition to her volunteer work, Mary and John have tried to stay involved in some way in their local parish, although not all of their children have embraced membership in the Church. "I made a promise that I'd help each one of them have a relationship with God," she says. Sometimes, she admits, that required stripping away the need to control, to judge. "Some of my kids could have been worshiping Our Lady of the Dairy Queen some Sundays, when I thought they were going to church," she laughs. "But I've tried to let go of the control and to be thankful for all they've taught me."

Mercy Association has provided a framework for ministry for this homemaker, mother, grandmother and full-time nurse to over 1,500 middle-school children. But this affiliation with the Sisters of Mercy is also the source of a rich spiritual journey. Association helped Mary recognize her ministry to herself, giving her the encouragement to seek a spiritual director. "Like many women, I've always found it easier to love others more than myself." Of her spiritual director, a Sister of Mercy, Mary says: "Her tender words – 'be still…wait…let go…move on…keep praying…' have touched my soul. They are Mercy received, so that I can become Mercy."

Two

Hans Hallundbaek
Maryknoll Affiliate

*"The whole mechanism of modern life is geared to a flight...
from spirit into the wilderness of neurosis."* Thomas Merton

Adapted from
From Singapore to Sing Sing ... and Back
by Hans Hallundbaek

Sitting in the parking lot outside the front gate of Sing Sing Correctional Facility in Ossining, New York, Hans Hallundbaek waits patiently. He has already waited over an hour to pick up his friend Ricco, who was to be released by noon.

He waits patiently, realizing the delay is nothing compared to the ten years Ricco, a former major drug dealer from New York City, has waited behind bars. It is also nothing in comparison to the seven years Hans Hallundbaek has spent in service work since a personal change made him leave a profitable business.

So he waits, watching the thirty-foot-high, scaling, gray walls draped with razor wire and dotted with ominous watchtowers. He waits to share with Ricco the incredible joy of freedom at last, of driving him back to his mother's home in the Bronx. He waits to do what friends do - share in each other's joy as well as sorrow and suffering.

"I'd met Ricco two years earlier in a privately funded, college-level educational program at Sing Sing," Hans explains. "We were both teaching about ministry in the program, he as an inmate who had earned a Master's degree in Theology, and I as a volunteer from the outside. We had been brought together by the common experience of a major life change."

Hans reflects on how the change which brought him to prison work cost him the friendship of those he used to work with in the business world. "They may listen politely," he says, "but they do not understand." Instead, this former engineer and international business consultant developed a whole new set of friends, mainly lay and ordained missionaries. "I can share with them on a much more profound level."

When Ricco finally comes out, he and Hans embrace while the gate slams shut behind him, signaling freedom has finally broken through. They drive away in silence, letting the experience sink in.

As they approach his mother's apartment building in the South Bronx, Ricco does not immediately rush to his waiting mother and girlfriend. Instead he looks up and down the battered, graffiti-infested street with boarded-up stores, broken windows, and litter and then turns to Hans with tears in his eyes, saying, "This is where our work begins."

There was a time when Hans did not think such change was possible. But he points to an interest in self-change that is increasingly evident in our society. Books on spiritual development are at the top of the best-seller list, and turning to angels is regularly suggested on primetime TV shows.

Hans describes himself as someone who had been living a hectic, driven, self-centered, fear-based lifestyle, globetrotting in the fast lane of international first-class business travel, luxury hotels, five-star restaurants and executive meeting rooms. What led him to trade this life for one of feeding homeless people on

New York streets, teaching inmates at maximum security prisons, and visiting poor people in remote villages in this country and abroad - all on a volunteer basis or compensated at a rate far below minimum pay?

His is not a story about a quick and miraculous burning bush experience leading to instant joy and happiness ever after. "Change for personal growth is a challenge to be approached with much respect," he cautions, "for it does not necessarily make life easier. But it does make life worth living on a profound level from where one never wants to return."

In retrospect, Hans realizes he was driven into a material, self-centered lifestyle from a poor and love-starved childhood in a desolate part of Europe. "Adding to this oppressive influence of my upbringing," he adds, "was the Nazi-German occupation of our country – Denmark – during my formative years from age five to ten.

"In my childhood, we hardly dared to whisper the word *freedom*, although it was a concept always in our hearts." When the wheels of change turned and the Danes were eventually freed from the German occupation, it was memorable for him. "I can still visualize, taste and smell how it felt that early spring evening of May 4, 1945, when the message of German surrender reached us over the hissing short-wave radio from BBC, London." Hans still recalls the spontaneous church bells, the people streaming out of their houses and dancing into the warm spring evening, then placing lit candles in their windows, as if forever to scare away the darkness. At the age of ten, freedom and liberation were concepts beginning to form in his consciousness.

Even though political and individual freedom had returned to his country, darkness still prevailed in spiritual form. "The oppressive influence of a fundamentalist Bible-thumping state church was prominent and preached a vengeful God threatening hell and damnation for sins."

Hans followed the mainstream through high school, college, engineering school, marriage, and family. But he began to see his choices as "vain attempts of finding freedom in a socially prescribed model by unquestioned submission to the establishment." Eventually he won a temporary freedom by shedding a bad marriage and moving to a country as far away as he could think of – Japan, the land of the rising sun. "In a culture totally different from western tradition, I was able to start anew and found freedom, at least for a while."

Relieved from the constraints of his Western upbringing, and invited into a radically different culture, Hans felt accepted more as a curiosity than as an individual expected to follow the rules of Japanese society. The result, he says, "was tremendous liberation, leading to growth materially, financially, and mentally. Life was good on all levels!"

Hans rose to the level of vice president of an American company, traveling not only over most of Japan, but subsequently into all the major countries of the Far East and South East Asia. Faraway destinations like Hong Kong, Bangkok, Singapore, Taipei, Kuala Lumpur and Manila, which had previously been dreams, now became regular places of business. So also did their first-class hotels, restaurants and entertainment spots.

Life in the fast lane continued for Hans for six years, with tremendous rewards. Then the law of the corporate structure, requiring adherence to a common denominator of mediocrity, sprang into effect. While his performance was exemplary, his independence was judged unsuitable for the company, and he was dismissed. "Why does good performance so often lead to envy and dismissal?" he wondered. He decided that only by working for himself could he feel truly free. His new wife, with him during the Far East experience, reluctantly agreed. Together they set out to establish an international marketing company, based upon their extensive contacts and experience.

They set aside six months and ten thousand dollars to test the idea and bought two airline discount tickets for around the world. For two months they traveled to every destination from London, Copenhagen, Zurich and Frankfurt, to Bangkok, Singapore, Penang, Seoul and Tokyo, returning with two clients on retainer and enough other projects to keep them busy for the next two years.

Over the next fifteen years, this venture proved close to what Hans had dreamed of in terms of freedom and independence. While working on worthwhile projects with good clients, the business grew and became the leading consulting and trading firm in its line of business. By 1990, the combined revenue had reached $2 million. It was the same year Hans decided to leave the business.

After almost thirty years in the business world, a new realization was slowly setting in. There had to be more to life than power, prestige, money, travel, gourmet restaurants, and material goods. Hans had experienced the excitement of owning a Jaguar XJ6, cruising a sailboat, and piloting a private plane. He had climbed Mount Fuji and done scuba diving in Hawaii, the Caribbean, and the Marinas Islands. He had run a marathon, skied the Austrian Alps, parasailed in Malaysia and visited five continents. "I knew there was much more to do along the same lines," he says, "but I also began to realize that lasting joy and happiness would not come from continuing to do the things advertised in the tourist brochures and the travel section of the newspaper."

As he started to ponder the deeper questions of life, such as *Who am I? Where am I?* and *Why am I here?* he quickly learned these apparently simple questions are dangerous. "Once they get under your skin, they will not let you go." Hans spent more and more time searching for that hidden reality. While continuing to travel extensively, he recognized travel as an excellent opportunity for soul searching. He came to grips with his fundamentalist upbringing, with the fact that he was "a latecomer in my family of three siblings all considerably older," realizing, he says, that "perhaps I had been a mistake and an embarrassment to my parents." This opened the floodgates to other realizations, such as the psychological oppression of living his formative years in an occupied country under Nazi-German control. "When I read the Eastern sage, Djwhal Khul, who said, 'Freedom is the birthright of every human being,' I knew there was a new reality of ultimate freedom awaiting if only I persevered. My spiritual journey was under way."

This led to the realization that being a consultant, however successful, was not really freedom. It meant only that instead of answering to one boss in a corporation, he now had to answer to various clients at any particular time. He came home to his wife and partner and announced he wanted to leave the business. A harrowing experience in Singapore where he had been hospitalized for three days against his will had convinced him of the fragility of freedom, and he vowed to continue his search at all levels.

"Relieved to see me back home, my wife decided to accept my decision to leave the business without much discussion," he recalls. "She took up the slack and continued our consulting practice, while encouraging me to pursue my new spiritual direction." During this time, Hans had also begun writing articles, in an effort to expose the exploitation he saw in many of the businesses he dealt with. When he succeeded in having his writing published, "I learned I had a writing voice, with potential to broadcast to a larger audience."

For two years, Hans explored a new and strange world, with visits to the Earth Summit in Rio, a United Nations social conference in Copenhagen, and to poor people in work camps in Nicaragua, Mississippi and Appalachia. He recalls them as "years of tremendous consciousness raising on issues of ecology, sustainability, poverty, and suffering. But I also witnessed hope against all odds."

Hans felt he needed to put his newfound insights into an academic context, so he attended the Maryknoll School of Theology where he earned a Master's Degree in Theology in 1994. He completed a Master of Divinity degree from New York Theological Seminary in 1997. "Years of rigorous study in these liberal, Christianity-based institutions gave me a much needed counterbalance to my childhood fundamentalism," he explains. "Besides a modern approach to theology, it taught me critical thinking, social analysis, and practical, biblical ways in which to develop a sustainable, just society across lines of gender, race, culture, and preferences."

Joining the Maryknoll Affiliate movement opened the door to the vast missionary network of the Maryknoll organization with fellowship and encouragement from others seeking to become servers of a new society. Hans found the Maryknoll organization with its strong focus on solidarity with the poor to be an invaluable support for his ministry. Association with like-minded individuals and observing ordained and lay missionaries in action in various parts of the world proved highly inspirational.

Whether it is working with prisoners or others in oppressed situations, Hans receives more than he could ever give. "The faith and hope of these prisoners, against all odds, is a constant humbling experience and strengthens my own resolve and faith." And sharing his ministry stories with his fellow Maryknoll Affiliates working in similar situations is a constant source of affirmation.

Years of tuition for education, books, and commuting costs took a heavy toll on family reserves. He was no longer able to go to exotic places for study and work camps for poor and marginalized people, who had become his primary focus of interest. However, the streets of New York proved to be a very valuable outlet, and through various organizations, he worked with homeless people in their need for food and clothing and for contact and communication with the rest of society.

Hans calls it "a fortunate coincidence" that he landed a job as volunteer teacher of theology and ethics at the infamous Sing Sing Correctional Facility. Here in the dungeons of a maximum-security prison for inmates with serious criminal records, he saw first hand the struggle and striving of the human spirit for change, growth, and reconciliation. "To be part of that transformation," he says, "proved to be more joyful and rewarding than all the globetrotting in the world."

To cover the cost of this new vocation, Hans had to find an income-producing job. Not wanting to go back to the business world, he chose limousine driving. Back and forth to the airports with business executives in stretch limos became his way of paying for schooling.

"While I was in the business world, my worst fear of failure had always been one day sinking to join the lines of limo drivers at the arrival gate, holding up a flimsy cardboard sign for Mr. Jones, or Mrs. Smith," he laughs. "Now I was there voluntarily, holding up that sign and not minding it at all." The job was flexible, gave lots of time for reading, reflection, and meditation, while driving an empty car or waiting for delayed flights. Besides, the conversations between business executives from the back seat of the limo were a constant reminder of his having made the right decision in leaving the shallow, material and empty world of business.

"In contrast, the seminary, homeless people on the streets, and the various prisoners I ministered to made it possible to address real, profound and meaningful issues." The issues dealt with struggle, survival, discrimination, poverty, oppression, and exploitation as well as growth, transformation, community, and hope. "The institutions at the bottom of the social ladder in a paradoxical way became the places that taught me the true way to freedom." Today, it seems obvious to Hans that we are all here for each other. "I consider it my calling to spend all my energy, training, and experience doing my small part in bringing humanity back from the edge towards a just and sustainable future." In his years of study, Hans has recognized the need for a universal sister/brotherhood of all human beings based upon love and compassion. "Until that unity is accomplished, I consider it my job to be a servant of those in need, and a provider of information and encouragement to those seeking to raise their awareness on these issues."

Hans is often asked whether he's achieved what he hoped for when he took the challenge of seeking freedom. "Definitely so. More importantly, I have realized that the challenge to seek freedom is much more than just a challenge. It is nothing less than an opportunity for excitement, joy and peace (and hard work), available to all of us."

Nine years after his last visit to Asia, Hans was recently on a five-week writing assignment to prisons and other social sore spots in Hong Kong, Taipei, Bangkok, Japan, Indonesia, the Philippines, and even Singapore. Reconnecting with familiar parts of the world in order to encourage social change rather than to conduct a profitable business deal proved rewarding for him. "I hope it will open the way for a return to globetrotting," he says, "but with a much different message and direction."

Three
Martina Kocher
Associate of the Dominican Sisters of Springfield, Illinois

Do not fear, for I am with you. I will bring your offspring from the east, from the west I will gather you. I will say to the north, "Give them up," and to the south, "Do not withhold; bring my sons from far away and my daughters from the end of the earth - everyone who is called by my name, whom I created for my glory, whom I formed and made."   *Isaiah 43:5-7*

*M*artina Kocher stands on the back porch of a stately redbrick building, Villa Maria Catholic Life Center, in Springfield, Illinois. The retreat center, sprawled across a lush lakefront edged by woods, is both her home and workplace. Surrounded by this beauty, the middle-aged woman with the wide smile and slight German accent, welcomes groups of men and women for weekend retreats, workshops and days of recollection. She is showing off the blazing tulips and sweet-smelling iris in her well-ordered garden, while she laughs about spending her weekends with scores of men.

Then her full face turns serious, recalling her first visit to the Center under less happy circumstances. It was 1986, and she had just separated from her husband of 26 years – his initiative. Her four children were out of high school, and for the first time, Martina was forced to support herself. "I told my parish priest about my college education in Germany as a home economics major," she recalls. The Catholic Diocese of Springfield had been looking for an activities director for a new retreat center – a recently converted seminary. The job sounded interesting, but it meant she would have to leave her familiar parish, give up her home, and move to a new city. "It was such a difficult decision," she says, recalling the devastation she felt, "but I didn't *dare* think of myself as broken. I had to be strong." Once she set foot on the grounds of Villa Maria, she said to herself, "This is my home. And it has to be a home for everyone who comes here, no matter how short or how long they stay."

Martina calls that job opportunity "a direct gift from God." She also credits her parish priest and Sister Phyllis Marie Schenk, a Dominican sister, who was the pastoral associate at the parish, for helping her to deal with the pain of divorce. "They walked with me during that difficult time. Now I realize how blessed and fortunate I was to have them." She also sees in retrospect how both her association with the Dominican sisters and the experience of divorce were preparing her for a greater work.

Martina's living room, in the east wing of the building, is large and sunny, with comfortable chairs and antique rockers. She explains that at one time it had been the chapel for a community of Franciscan sisters who had lived and worked there when it was a seminary. Along one wall stands a collection of music, books, and memorabilia; another wall is crowded with pampered plants. This is her room for journal writing or meditation; sometimes others join her for common prayer. She calls it her "healing room" and it is warm and inviting.

Healing is something Martina has been trying to do for a long time. "My life has not been easy," she says, hinting at a childhood scarred by war. She tends to understate the pain she experienced as a five-year-old, fleeing to Alsace with her pregnant mother, her sister and brother, to escape bombing in her hometown of Karlsrühe, Germany, during World War II. Then

Allied Forces ordered them to an internment camp in southern France, where the death rate was almost fifty percent, where no young children had ever survived, and where food was so scarce that they ate the weeds that sprang up around the prison camp.

Martina recalls lying near death from tuberculosis, saved by her mother who refused to send her to the prison camp hospital. "I brought three children with me," her mother had declared, "and I will leave with three children." Through a prisoner exchange, she and her mother, sister, and brother were finally able to return to Karlsrühe, where they found that seventy percent of their town had been destroyed. Their apartment building had been bombed, and there was no glass available to replace windows, so they had to live in the cellar for several years. Her youngest sister was born there, without her father, who, they learned, had been killed while trying to escape a firebombing.

She explains that her mother's faith was tested to the point that she could no longer go to church. And she remembers her mother's words, "A good God would never have let this happen." Martina's own religious upbringing ended at age seventeen and failed to provide her with a way to deal with the horror of war. Her pain remained buried.

Music became a refuge. While her mother could not afford to give her music lessons, she took her to free concerts where Martina soaked up Bach and Brahms. In fact, it was music that brought her and her husband together. She was eighteen when they met at a music festival, where she sang in a civic choir and he in his college chorus. Two years later, they married and then lived in Illinois, where he was attending graduate school. While she continued to develop her appreciation for music (she still sings with the Springfield Symphony Chorus), her interest in the Roman Catholic Church wavered.

Martina defines her faith in the years to follow as "lukewarm." Involved in the Civil Rights Movement during the 1960s, she did not see the Church as relevant. When her children were of school age and attended parish religion classes, she realized that she wanted to know more about her own faith. "I took out books, studied catechetics, read the Scriptures, and wrote in my journal," she says. This eventually led to her teaching Parish School of Religion classes.

Since 1986, as the director of the retreat center, Martina has had many opportunities for spiritual growth. During a retreat in 1987, she found herself telling her director about the pain of her childhood, all the while insisting, "It isn't relevant." But as she read a passage from Chapter 43 of Isaiah and rewrote it in her own words, she says, "I could see that God was gathering all the broken pieces which that war had scattered for me." She wrote: *From wherever you have been, I have gathered your pieces and brought them to this place, to make you whole.*

For several years, her spiritual growth and healing continued, but she explains, "There was no structure to this growth." Then, through the invitation of her spiritual director, a Dominican sister, the structure she had been searching for came in the form of association. In 1990, she said *yes* to the invitation to become an associate of the Springfield Dominicans. After a year of preparation with the sisters, she wrote a statement that publicly committed her to follow the spirit and charism of the Dominican Order.

The particular spirit of the order "just felt right to me," she proclaims, explaining that this involved teaching and preaching the Word of God, offering hospitality, spending time in prayer, and supporting the community. "It was a perfect fit," Martina says, as she committed herself to offer hospitality to all who visit Villa Maria. "I'm the mother of a very large house!" she chuckles. She was already preaching and teaching the Good News through weekend retreats, where she continues to learn more about her faith. And as for prayer, she says, "Every time I go to my flower bed, it's prayer."

Although she has to miss some of the Sunday study days open to associates at the Dominican Motherhouse because of retreats in progress, she looks forward to visiting the sisters once a week for evening prayer and supper. At first, she looked upon association as a gift from the sisters to her, but eventually she realized that her going there was good for the sisters, too. "I thought I was receiving the gift, but I could see that they were very happy to see me," she smiles, "and I realized that association is a two-way street." She adds, "Of course, their side of the street may be a bit wider than mine!"

It was the Dominican sisters who nudged her toward her special ministry to the divorced. As a divorced Catholic involved in retreat work, Martina was struck by the fact that divorced and separated Catholics rarely participated in the retreats; and if they did, they felt no one else could understand their pain. They felt rejected by the Church and found it hard to discuss their situation, which only increased their sense of isolation. "Something should be done for these divorced and separated Catholics," Martina thought, especially for those who hadn't been as lucky as she to find support from individuals like Sister Phyllis. But it wasn't until 1994, when it came time to renew her commitment, that she became conscious that *she* was the one who had to *do something.*

In preparation for her recommitment to association with the Dominican sisters, her spiritual director asked Martina if she wanted to change her commitment statement. "No," she answered. "It still works." The sister smiled and said, "I think you may want to take a day of prayer before you recommit." Martina spent the day at the Dominican Sisters' Renewal Center, and by mid-afternoon, it had become clear to her that she must add another point to her statement. That evening she stood before the sisters, associates, and invited guests. In addition to the teaching, hospitality, prayer, and attention to community she had promised, she also dedicated herself "to work actively in ministry to the divorced and separated people in our Church." She credits a Dominican sister's love and compassion with helping her to survive the devastation of her own divorce. "I felt compelled to help others," she says. "You have to give what you've received. It doesn't serve a purpose unless you can pass it on."

Then she leans back with her hearty laugh. "I had no idea how I was going to accomplish this. But we all prayed, sisters and associates, that we might find ways of realizing the ministry." Eventually a new movement called DASK, Divorced and Separated *Koinonia* (Fellowship), was born. Using the *Koinonia* retreat format, an already existing inter-faith program, which was an offshoot of the Cursillo movement, and Teens Encounter Christ, Martina tailored the model to the unique experiences of the divorced Catholic.

19

A year later, in 1995, the first DASK was offered, with Martina as rector or leader, and with the whole community of Dominican sisters behind her with their prayers and support. "With DASK, we didn't need icebreakers, like on other weekend retreats," she explains. "These people were anxious to begin the healing process!" The participants introduced themselves, telling how long they had been separated or divorced. For some of them, it was the first time they had spoken the words aloud. "It was a very powerful moment, a first step toward trusting again," she says.

For Martina, although the hurt of divorce will always be there, "it assumes its proper place, by the grace of God." But when it happened, she remembers saying to her pastor, "I look for Martina, and there's nobody there." Through her loneliness and pain, she has come to understand the Paschal mystery, the truth about death and resurrection. "When I realized God was in all of it, I could become grateful for all of it." She cherishes the words of Jesus: "Don't you know that just as you are with me in my loneliness, so I am with you in yours."

"The sisters have truly been partners in my ministry," she explains, recalling how, during her first DASK, she called them several times a day for assistance. "I think I wanted to be sure they knew I was out there struggling!" she laughs. "But seriously, I would never put on one of these retreats without the prayers of the sisters. They pray. Then I tell them how it went. Our partnership is very real."

On a wall in her hallway are photos of her three sons and one daughter. Snapshots of her grandsons sit framed near her computer. While her family visits often and stays connected through email and telephone, they are involved in establishing their own lives. "The sisters have become another family," she says. "Association is somewhere I'm very glad to be, and I know the sisters are glad to have me."

Martina feels the support of the sisters, but she also appreciates the challenge that being an associate offers. "Not challenge in the way of judgment," she says, "but in the sense that they remind me to go out to my ministry; that there is work to be done."

Every four years, Springfield Dominican Associates decide to recommit, but for Martina, a lifetime commitment would fit just fine. "I like the steadfastness and the continuity of belonging, the sense of permanence." One thing she knows for sure, she would not have started her ministry to divorced and separated Catholics without the encouragement from the sisters. And with the sisters as her partners, she has been able to minister to hundreds of individuals, like her, who come to Villa Maria to heal their lives.

Four

Isabel Guadiz Tobey
Associate of Sisters of the Incarnate Word

But you are merciful to all, for you can do all things, and you overlook people's sins, so that they may repent. For you love all things that exist .... You spare all things, for they are yours, who love the living.   Wisdom 11:23-26

A small child scrapes the sand with her favorite toy, a discarded sardine can. Shaded by the house that stands on stilts, she has found solitude from her eight brothers and sisters. After dinner, her mother will gather the children for night prayer. Darkness will fall in the little Philippine village, and without electricity, the children will go to bed.

"How, from that little girl, did I get to where I am today?" Isabel Guadiz Tobey wonders. Her journey – from that remote village to an affluent Cleveland suburb, from poor child to successful pediatrician – is a story of anger and confusion, faith and devotion, compassion and acceptance. "Without the support and friendship of the sisters," Isabel beams a smile, "I don't know where I would be."

The anger and confusion began when she was very young. She was already noticing her mother's pain and humiliation, stemming from her father's frequent infidelity. As she grew older, she would hear the gossip about her half-sisters and brothers – a cultural taboo her mother bore silently. In Manila, her father's merchant job prospered, but the shame haunted Isabel, and the resentment deepened. "We didn't have money for shoes or clothes," she recalls as the fourth of nine children, "because my father was actually supporting thirteen other children born to other women. I hated his sin and resented what I saw as neglect." She admits she was a difficult child. "I was rebellious, especially in my teens. I didn't respect my father's lies or my mother's submissiveness."

In spite of the family's poverty, her parents had set aside enough money for one of the children to go to medical school, and Isabel, for as long as she could remember, had dreamed of being a doctor. She felt relief each time her older siblings decided against medical school. While she begged her parents to let her go, Isabel also felt drawn to the Salesian Sisters who had educated her in elementary school. She helped them teach catechism to the younger children, and was a member of the mission club. "I loved the sisters," she recalls. "They were my friends, and secretly I thought I should join them so I could do penance for my father's sins."

But when she revealed to her parents that she wanted to be a nun, they replied that the order of sisters would never allow her to be a nun *and* a doctor. "I prayed to God, asking what I should do." After a short time in the sisters' convent as an aspirant, she still felt she needed to atone for her father's sins, but she could see that the religious life was not her calling.

Between high school and medical school, a young man began courting her. Her father disapproved of the boy. Isabel decided that marrying him secretly before a Justice of the Peace would spite her father. "I was too young to know if I loved the boy or not," she says. "But he seemed to like me a lot, and he wanted to marry me." The boy, a native of Guam, lacked education and the advantages of a stable home life, and Isabel felt compassion for him. "I was very confused, and I resisted my parents' advice and their wishes for a Church wedding," she says. Eventually, believing being married in the Church would assure the marriage's success, she agreed.

She entered medical school as a young married woman, and almost immediately the trouble began. Her new husband could find work only in Guam and would return home to her after long absences. During visits home he drank heavily and was abusive. "I thought it was my fault," she sighs. "I thought I could change him. I believed that it was up to me to make the marriage work." Within the first two years, two daughters were born. "I took care of the babies and continued to go to medical school," she recalls. "My constant prayer was: *God, where are you? You've got to help me with this.*" After five years, at the age of 23, she had completed her undergraduate classes and was ready to begin a residency in pediatrics.

An older sister living in Cleveland, Ohio, encouraged Isabel to come there to complete her medical training. "I was determined to keep the marriage together, in spite of my husband's alcoholism and abuse," she says. They moved to Cleveland in 1977, and soon their third child, a son, was born. In three years, Isabel began private practice as a pediatrician, desperate to support her family. Five years later, a fourth child, a girl, was born. Isabel believes her faith in God, her devotion to the Virgin Mary, and her willingness to stay connected through prayer sustained her during those years.

Ten years passed. Her pediatric practice had begun to prosper, but she felt spiritually and emotionally bankrupt. Still carrying the anger and resentment of her childhood, and unable to stop her husband from verbal and physical abuse of her and their children, her constant prayer became, *God, I don't like this cross you're giving me. Why don't you take it?* One day she felt sure she heard an answer, *I've already done that.* A few days later in her office, the mother of an infant she was treating asked her about the statue of the Christ crowned with thorns, and the different images of Mary in her office. "We shared a similar faith experience," Isabel recalls. "She told me about her association with the Sisters of the Incarnate Word in Cleveland, and she invited me to consider becoming an associate myself." Isabel accepted the invitation as an answer to her prayer.

Being with the sisters in prayer and community was exactly what Isabel needed, not only to satisfy a lifelong spiritual hunger and to nurture her medical practice, but also to give her the support she needed to deal with her abusive marriage and heal the anger of her childhood.

The charism of the Sisters of the Incarnate Word – to live out the Beatitudes in daily life – appealed to Isabel on many levels. But as a person who had placed great value on doing everything with efficiency, both at home and in her medical practice, she was touched by the sisters' practice of being the image of God to others rather than simply performing actions. "Being more like Christ, living the Gospel of love," she says, "is what I learned from the sisters."

During a year of formation in the associate program with her contact person, Sister Mary Ellen Ryan, Isabel met the sisters in the small community and learned more about their ministry of teaching and working with people who are poor. Together they shared their faith experiences and daily common prayer.

"I meet so many people every day – babies and their mothers, especially – and as an associate, I can be an extension of the Incarnate Word, the Word made flesh, to all those people!" Every three years, since 1987, Isabel has renewed her covenant to follow the order's charism by living the Gospel through the Beatitudes, and by joining with the community in prayer.

Inside the front door of her inviting home, Isabel proudly displays a large family portrait, taken at the wedding of her oldest daughter, Michelle. She points out a small wrinkled man, and a broad smile lights her high cheek bones and round face. "I have forgiven him," she says of her father. "With the help of the sisters, I was able first to forgive the angry child inside myself. Then," she continues, "I could forgive my father his weakness."

It was also through the support of the Incarnate Word Sisters that Isabel was finally able to end her abusive marriage. Trying to discern whether or not she should file for divorce, the sisters encouraged her to make a weekend retreat. "I prayed to God, saying I only wanted to do His will," she remembers. The other retreatants supported her in her decision to seek dissolution of the marriage. "My husband was not a bad person, but his addiction turned him into a violent man," she says. "Now I am trying to help my four children heal from their own pain."

Exactly three years after receiving an annulment from her first marriage, she was married to John Tobey, who had been one of the participants of that weekend retreat. Raised an Italian Catholic, John had been so supportive of Isabel's association with the Incarnate Word Sisters that he also decided to become an associate.

Isabel finds association supports her healing profession, describing her work with infants and children as "graced moments" when she sees the image of God. "I could never violate the trust put in me. I know, as an Associate of the Incarnate Word, that I am better able to be the healing face of God." Also, she says, her association gives her the strength to speak honestly, to seek justice, and to be bold in her expression of truth, with the help of the Holy Spirit.

Isabel has many stories about her deepening awareness of God's presence through her work as a doctor. While working nights at a local hospital, in order to pay for her daughter's college tuition, she passed by the room of a terminally ill woman, crying out alone in her bed, her arms restrained. "I went into her dark room and held her hand, trying to soothe her crying." The woman opened her eyes and whispered, "Please don't leave me." Isabel told her she would stay as long as she could, and that she would pray with her. "I couldn't help but think of Jesus' words to his disciples in the Garden of Gethsemane: *Won't you watch one hour with me?*" As Isabel prayed, the woman's labored breathing gradually calmed, and she fell into a deep sleep. Before leaving the hospital in the morning, Isabel checked in to find that her condition had stabilized.

A young mother named Cathy occupies a special place in Isabel's heart. A woman who has suffered from abuse and abandonment, Cathy is raising two sons without the help of her ex-husband. "I could identify with her anger," Isabel remembers, "and I prayed that God would show me how to help her." Cathy had challenged her, saying that Isabel's life was easy; how could she appreciate her hardships? "I have been – and still can be – as mean as you, Cathy," Isabel told her. "The only difference is I have the love of God in my life." Isabel believes her association with the sisters gives her the grace and power to speak truth.

Being an associate appeals to Isabel, who likes to describe herself as a "monkette." At first you have to look hard to see her contemplative side. Just under five feet, this human dynamo swirls through a tour of her busy office, then swings by to pick up her youngest daughter, Anna. As she sits in her living room, talking about her spiritual journey, one is aware of her energy, the humor that dances in her dark eyes, and the love that spreads across her face in a broad smile.

The seeds of her contemplation become more evident as she begins to explain the importance of her association with the Sisters of the Incarnate Word. "I have learned to be more faithful to the Word of God." Her dark gentle eyes fill with tears. "I know now that I am God's child forever. That was the gift given to me at Baptism. But association makes it more clear," she explains. "Being an associate has made me more able to express my Baptism, because the sisters and I can speak the same language." Her eyes widen. "You see? I am able to reclaim the fact of my Baptism in God. Isn't that wonderful?"

On a tiny altar in her kitchen, a book of daily prayers – the Abbey Psalter used by the Trappist Monks – is open to Psalm 67. This morning ritual puts her and her family in spiritual union with the monks at prayer. The Word of God becomes incarnate through the life of a tiny Philippino child who has traveled all the way to Cleveland to journey in association with a group of about fifty Sisters of the Incarnate Word.

What will happen to this small group of aging sisters? "Oh, we'll continue their work," Isabel doesn't hesitate. "This partnership between the sisters and the laity is all the work of the Holy Spirit. The Word will continue to be spoken in the world." Her dark eyes dance, and she laughs again. "You see? In Baptism, we are all members of the Incarnate Word!"

Five

Dee Nelson
Associate of the Dominican Sisters
of Springfield, Illinois

*And what does God require of you but to do justice, and to love
kindness, and to walk humbly with your God?*   Micah 6:8

"*A*s far as I knew," says Dee Nelson, "I had
never met a prostitute." What, then, called her to decide to walk
the downtown streets of her hometown *with* them? Dee was in
her mid-forties. It was 1981. She had noticed a newspaper article
about a Franciscan priest ministering to prostitutes on the south
side of Chicago. "I was planning to visit a friend who was studying
at the Catholic Theological Union on Chicago's South Side," she
recalls, "so I tucked the article in my bag to show her." Dee was
surprised when the same priest from the article joined them at
their lunch table. "I asked him about his ministry," she says, "and
he invited me to walk with him through the red-light district – he
referred to it as *The Stroll* - to see what it was like." She declined.
"It was November – too cold," she shrugs. "But I told him I might
come back in the spring."

Months later, Dee's curiosity and a sense of adventure
lured her back to Chicago to take *The Stroll*. This brief immersion

29

left her with an unexpected sensitivity toward women in prostitution. "I started noticing newspaper and magazine articles about prostitution," she says. At the same time, she was puzzled by her interest. But that interest only grew, so a few months later, she decided to spend a night at a Chicago shelter for prostitutes called Genesis House, founded by Edwina Gateley.

Later, during a trip to St. Louis, she met Sister Agnes Marie Baer, a former high-school principal who had convinced law enforcement officials in St. Louis to allow her to provide academic tutoring in lieu of incarceration for women convicted of prostitution.

Dee is quick to point out that she is a very ordinary person – a middle-aged, stay-at-home mother of four, whose limited use of her elementary teacher certification included a few years of substitute teaching. She raised her children in the same turn-of-the-century home on Walnut Street where she had grown up, in mid-American Springfield, Illinois, in the shadow of the State Capitol, surrounded by sites where young Abraham Lincoln practiced law.

There was one thing, though, that distinguished her backyard from her neighbors' – a large swimming pool. "Put me near water," says this tall woman of Norwegian stock, with a gray pixie cut and blinking eyes, "and I'm at home." Children flock to her summer swim lessons. "Close to one thousand children in Springfield over twenty-five years," she beams, "and there's always a waiting list."

In fact, it was swimming that drew her to a closer association with the Dominican Sisters of Springfield. Not that she was a stranger to the sisters. Her grandmother had been a friend of the founding members of the order of nuns in Springfield, and her mother had begun studying under the sisters at age four. Dee's sister had belonged to the order for seventeen years, and Dee herself had been educated by them.

When she learned that the elderly sisters at the Dominican Motherhouse were having difficulty using their pool, she remembers thinking: "I could help them with that!" She set aside a few hours on Monday and Friday evenings, volunteering to teach them water aerobics. "That was fifteen years ago," she smiles, "and I'm still at it."

The prostitutes she couldn't forget overshadowed her calm, ordinary, even idyllic life as housewife, mother, volunteer, and friend of the sisters. Dee now knows by heart the statistics that in 1982 had shocked her. Ten million people in the United States are involved in the phenomenon of prostitution. Ninety eight percent of the women suffer from chemical addictions. Over ninety percent are victims of physical and/or sexual abuse. All suffer from low self-esteem. The average age of a woman entering prostitution is fourteen years. Few complete secondary schooling, and few possess job skills. "I felt compassion for these prostitutes," she explains. "Chronologically they were adults, but their childhood had been stolen from them, mostly by their fathers, uncles, brothers, grandfathers or close friends – their supposed caregivers." She began to wonder whether she herself might have turned to drugs or alcohol to numb the pain, had she been raped by her father or grandfather since age three or six.

"But what could I do?" she shrugged. She tucked her compassion away, busying herself with her family, her aging mother who had come to live with them, her swimming lessons, her two evenings a week with the Dominican sisters, and another volunteer job running a used clothing store sponsored by the Catholic Diocese of Springfield. Then in 1985, a young woman in prostitution was fatally shot on the railroad tracks a few blocks from the State Capitol and her home. "I was haunted by the feeling that, if I'd done something for the Springfield women in prostitution, as Edwina Gateley in Chicago and Sister Agnes Marie in St Louis had done," she says, "maybe that young woman would not have been killed."

Recalling Sister Agnes Marie's tutoring service in St. Louis, Dee decided that, with her education background, she could tutor the prostitutes of Springfield. Catholic Charities, a social service agency sponsored by the Springfield Catholic Church, gave Dee their blessing. But she dropped the idea when it became obvious that she'd have to walk the streets in the worst part of her hometown in order to find her potential students. A middle-aged housewife with children still living at home, she was not prepared to do that.

"For two years, I tried to still the voice of God calling me to *do something* for these women." She strokes the adoring head of her mixed-breed dog, Clyde, as she recounts the struggle. *"Did God really want me to walk the streets?* I wondered." Then Dee was given what she clearly saw as a sign. It came from the Dominican sisters she had known since childhood. "The community had just initiated an associate program, and they were inviting anyone interested to apply. I was the first associate to join," she states matter-of-factly. "I had decided that I would dedicate one year to walking the streets of Springfield, and I would ask the sisters to be my companions in prayer."

The Dominican sisters agreed to partner with her. "I asked to be an associate with the express intention of having the prayers of the sisters behind me, as I launched my private mission of streetwalking," she says. In early October of 1991, armed with the prayers of the sisters, filled with compassion for these oppressed women, and believing she could help them by giving them the gift of education, this middle-aged housewife set out on a whole new journey.

What did her husband and children think? What about her aging mother, who had lived with the family for over fifteen years, and whose strong personality had often made Dee defy her, rather than seek her mother's approval? "I didn't tell them," she says flatly. "They wouldn't have approved. And besides, I didn't want to worry them." Her lips curl in a sly smile as she explains that the sisters kept her secret. "I was already going to the Motherhouse on Mondays and Fridays," she explains. "So after I worked with the sisters in their pool, I'd ask them to pray for me while I drove to the red light district and parked my car on Sixth Street. From 9 to 10 p.m., I walked six blocks in one direction, crossed the street, then walked six blocks back to my car."

She handed out printed cards advertising her tutoring services to the suspicious young women. Yet once they became accustomed to Dee's presence, they began to treat her with respect and politeness. "No one was ever rude to me," she says. "I never worried, because I felt that, with the sisters praying, I was under God's protection." At times she would ask herself, *What in the world are you doing down here?* But her answer was always the same, *I'm not here because I want to be, I'm here because I'm called to be.*

A local charity promised her a room where she could tutor the women, should anyone accept her offer. Because she did not want to jeopardize her family, she had a separate phone line installed at home. During the year she had set aside for streetwalking, the phone rang twice. Both were wrong numbers.

Then, with two weeks left to go in the year, just as she was ready to surrender her mission and get on with her life, a local TV station approached her and eventually followed her on her "stroll" down Sixth Street. The airing of that TV program on prostitution led to an open forum in the city of Springfield. Following that, a group of individuals banded together to form what eventually became PORA (Positive Options, Referrals and Alternatives), a not-for-profit organization incorporated in 1993. And Dee found herself – a fish out of water – running a corporation.

She was joined in her streetwalking by a small group of volunteers. She also started a weekly support group for female inmates at the Sangamon County Jail, which still meets. "What do you need most?" she asked the prostitutes. "Safe housing," they told her. Dee's strong face wrenches with pain when she remembers the women in jail, weeping with the knowledge that, once they were released, their pimps would be waiting for them. Without knowing how she would pay for it, Dee began looking for a suitable home for these women.

What she found was an abandoned two-story building that had once been a corner bar and "speakeasy" – one of the many built in Springfield, before prohibition, to support a local brewery. Next she had to go looking for funding. "The Dominican sisters had been the spiritual backbone of my mission," Dee insists, "but now they were prepared to give more than their prayers to my mission." They dipped into a special fund to provide seed money. Then Dee learned from a local member of the School Sisters of Notre Dame of the St. Louis Province that they were accepting applications for grants. She had ten days to write a proposal – something she knew nothing about.

"My son bought me a computer and gave me a crash course on how to use it." She shakes her head in amazement at this part of the story. "I sat up in my third floor attic night after night writing grant proposals and filling out legalistic documents," she runs her thick fingers through her white hair. "Clyde would lie at my feet, patiently waiting for his evening walk around the block." Sometimes the dog had to wait until one or two in the morning, but his faithfulness was always rewarded. While Clyde reveled in the smells and sights in the streets, available to him at the end of his leash, Dee fingered the rosary beads she had tucked in her pocket. "I was caught in a foreign environment for which I was not trained or prepared," she says, leaning forward in her chair to make sure this part is understood. "I relied *totally* on the prompting of the Holy Spirit and the prayers of the sisters, and I prayed constantly for discernment."

On August 11, 1997, the first resident moved into the PORA building, which can house up to six women, with one living room, one bath, and three bedrooms, all on the second floor. The first floor included an office, a space for a small printing business, and sleeping arrangements for a night supervisor. From the beginning, Dee recounts, the nonprofit organization not only managed to stay out of debt, but had assets in excess of $200,000. Dee painted her favorite words on the front window of the building: "God is Good!"

Dee wants others to know about this transformed tavern. Whenever she leads a tour, she points out the copy machine, computers, files, and stacks of printed material taking up the tiny office space on the first floor. It comprises ABBA, the printing business that helps support the house, and at the same time, provides job training for the women. Behind the office and galley kitchen, there is an efficiency room where a volunteer spends the night, providing round-the-clock supervision. Dee points to photos of a room without a floor, another without a ceiling, showing the transformation she and hundreds of volunteers helped accomplish with the old tavern.

On the second floor, a television blares in the living room, and there is laughter and the smell of fish frying from the eat-in kitchen. Newly renovated bedrooms are decorated with posters and patchwork quilts. A toddler sleeps in the arms of his mother, as she talks about how she lives for these Sunday visits with him, and how hard it is to give him back to her sister until next week. The four young women residents tell us they thank God every day for PORA and Miss Dee.

One might expect Dee to be proud of her accomplishments. She shrugs and sinks her hands into the pockets of her jeans. "I don't feel much of anything," she tries to explain. She says she received awards, but the plaques are somewhere on a shelf. "It's nice, but awards never made the work any easier. Maybe this wouldn't have been as difficult for someone else – someone more suited to public work."

In the two years since the home opened, and in spite of support services such as counseling and job training, success stories have been few and guarded, because the pimp is always "out there" waiting, Dee says. "That's the way it is with us," one woman told her, after Dee watched her return to the man who abused her. Are those Dee's darkest hours? She thinks long and hard. "No. Those would have to be the board meetings." Dee often feels she should have stayed in the swimming pool where navigating came easy for her. Seven years after she had begun her streetwalking, after ripping out plaster and stripping woodwork in the deteriorating building, after troubleshooting situations she never could have imagined, she stepped down as PORA's director in order to give herself some distance. Contention and disagreement among the trustees on the PORA board prompted her withdrawal from everyday management as director of the home, although she serves as a board member. "I know, and God knows, what I was called to do," she says quietly. "I did it. The future is in God's hands."

Each week she continues to visit the women in jail, who tell her, "I saw you walking the street. Sometimes I felt you were the only one who cared."

Although Dee has stepped down from managing the shelter, she is already eyeing the property next door, which someone has offered to PORA. "They're asking too much," she says, "but the way I envision it, if we could put the offices and printing business next door," she points to a dilapidated frame house, "then the women could have more privacy...the way it should be." Of course, it all depends on finding the money. "Maybe writing more grants," she groans.

Association with the Dominican sisters continues to be a cornerstone of Dee's life. Besides the evenings she spends helping the elderly sisters exercise in their swimming pool, she meets regularly with the community to celebrate feasts and gather in prayer. She offers her prayers and material support to the sisters living among the poor in Springfield. But it's the partnership of prayer this housewife of simple faith formed with the Dominican women in 1990 that remains strong. "I never would have gone out on the streets without the sisters."

The neediest women in Springfield, Illinois – the prostitutes – whether they realize the importance and power of that association partnership or not, are glad Dee Nelson decided to walk the streets with them.

Six

Don and Mary Ellen Kreilkamp

Companions to the Missionaries
of the Precious Blood

I do not count my life of any value to myself, if only I may finish my course and the ministry that I received from the Lord Jesus, to testify to the good news of God's grace .... In all this I have given you an example that by such work we must support the weak, remembering the words of the Lord Jesus, for he himself said, "It is more blessed to give than to receive."   Acts of the Apostles 20:24, 35

"*A*s a Montessori teacher, I knew the world didn't revolve around us," says Mary Ellen Kreilkamp, as she bustles around her sunny kitchen preparing lunch. "Besides, I've always wanted to travel," she chuckles. Mary Ellen is referring to what motivated her and her husband Don to follow the call as missionaries. They *have* seen the world, especially after four missions to Africa, with side trips all over Europe. They were nearly packed and ready for their fifth trip to Tanzania, as Companions to the Missionaries of the Precious Blood (C.PP.S.) when they were told by the Fathers they would not be able to return. The Precious Blood community had just lost one of its American priests to a fatal heart attack in Africa. And since Don had been diagnosed with a serious heart condition following their last trip, the fathers felt the dangers to his health were too great. "The mission at Morogoro, where we were working, is so remote," Don explained, "that there is no way I could have gotten medical help in an emergency."

"We were devastated," says Mary Ellen. She arranges the bowls of homemade chicken-vegetable soup on a table set with a bright tablecloth, fresh daffodils and blue delft candlesticks. She has baked bread and prepared a pineapple upside down cake. "Oh, the pineapples," she sighs, "such good pineapples in Africa. I miss it all so much."

The tall, soft-spoken professor and his welcoming wife had traveled to Africa, guided by the traditions and spirituality of St. Gaspar del Bufalo, the founder of the Missionaries of the Precious Blood. During the fourteenth century, Gaspar, a parish priest, had preached and assisted the poor people of Rome and became known for his compassion and peace-making missions.

The seeds that drew them to become Companions to the Missionaries of the Precious Blood took root in the small college town of Rensselaer, Indiana. Mary Ellen had worked as a secretary at St. Joseph College in Rensselaer, sponsored by the Missionaries of the Precious Blood, helping to put her first husband through college. He was later killed in an automobile accident while they were living in Australia, where he was earning a Ph.D. in oceanography. As a widow with three children, she returned to Rensselaer to pursue studies in Montessori education at St. Joseph. "It was a difficult time for me," recalls Mary Ellen, "and the college became my community." There she met Don, who had come to teach philosophy at St. Joseph, after twenty years as a teacher and member of the Capuchin Fathers, a Franciscan Order. He had recently sought and received a dispensation from his vows and was teaching as a lay person.

"A teacher friend introduced us," says Mary Ellen remembering their first date. Don smiles and touches her hand. "God spoke to me through Mary Ellen." In 1971 they were married. Their stories overlap as they tell about their six-bedroom

Victorian home in Rensselaer where Mary Ellen opened her own Montessori School. They talk about how their family of five grew with a daughter born to them a year later and then an Amerasian son adopted in 1975. Stories unfold about the exchange students over the years – twenty in all – who came to stay with them, offering babysitting in exchange for room and board. World-renowned writers and activists speaking in Don's humanism course – as well as speakers from the Catholic Worker Movement and the International Peace Bureau – usually stayed at their home.

Don's call to missionary life manifested itself during the twenty-six years that he taught philosophy at St. Joseph College. Every seven years he was granted a leave from college teaching, and they traveled because, he explains, "We felt the kids needed to experience the real world outside our nice small town." In 1984 they interviewed with Maryknoll, hoping to spend their year's leave in Africa. But there were no English-speaking schools for their two children still in elementary school.

Instead, they became part of a community at a halfway house for recovering drug addicts in the New York Hudson River Valley. "We shared meals, took turns cooking, helped with the farm, even painted the house," says Mary Ellen. Not long after they moved in, they lost the renters who had been their livelihood. "Without our income," adds Don, "we had to live on food stamps." With government cheese and cracked eggs, Mary Ellen became the *Queen of Quiche.* "We couldn't eat quiche for years after that," she says. She also recalls once having to feed an unexpected crowd of visitors. "All we had was condensed milk and a handful of potatoes," she laughs. "But I made a potato soup that just seemed to multiply miraculously – like the loaves and fishes." It was that experience at the halfway house – living each day trusting in God's providence – that convinced Don and Mary Ellen that some day they would devote more of their time as missionaries to those less fortunate.

The Precious Blood fathers had established a tradition of associating lay people with their various missions. In 1990, Father Denny Kinderman, a priest of the Precious Blood Community at St. Joseph College, invited Don and Mary Ellen to join them in a deeper relationship as companions, another term for associates.

During a year of discernment they joined the Precious Blood fathers frequently at Mass and prayer, and they enjoyed being part of C.PP.S. community functions. "As teachers and members of the St. Joseph College community," says Don, "we were already sharing in part of their mission."

During the next few years, as the last of their children went off to college and they neared their retirement, Don and Mary Ellen began praying to St. Gaspar for guidance on what their new missionary work might be. Don, a student of the Russian language, was interested in going to Russia. But during a series of conversations with the Precious Blood Moderator General, Father Anton Loipfinger, and his associate, Father Gennaro Cespites, both visiting St. Joseph College from Italy, Don became convinced he was needed in Africa. "They were starting a seminary for native Africans at St. Gaspar's College, Morogoro [pop. 120,000], in central eastern Tanzania," says Don, "and they needed a philosophy professor!"

At the Provincial Assembly of the Missionaries of the Precious Blood in 1993, Don and Mary Ellen made a commitment to become missionaries by working in the African mission of the society. Arriving in Dar es Salaam on New Year's Day, 1994, they brought a cargo container of much-needed supplies, including books gleaned from the St. Joseph College library. "With me teaching and Mary Ellen cataloging all the books for their library," recalls Don, "the seminary won early accreditation from the Urbania University in Rome."

As the first lay missionary Companions of the Missionaries of the Precious Blood, Don and Mary Ellen lived in the College of St. Gaspar, praying and sharing in the daily life and work of the college's seminarians and priests.

Making the trip to Africa involved some hardships, including covering some of their own travel expenses. They made the decision to sell their big house. Following a floor plan they had seen in an Indiana State Park lodge, Don hired a builder to construct a new smaller home while they were away. They also had to leave behind their grown children and six grandchildren, although their youngest daughter, Emmy, a theatre major, made one trip with them, teaching and producing plays in the seminary.

The experience took a toll on their health. In spite of preventive medication, Mary Ellen almost died from one of her three bouts with malaria. Don escaped malaria until the fourth year. Both suffer side effects – problems with eyesight – from a drug taken to combat the disease. But Don's greatest health risk came in the form of a silent heart attack, which left him with a weakened heart – the reason they could not return.

Faced with the fact that they would not be returning to Africa, Don decided to act on a desire he'd had for some time. "I was beginning to realize that, instead of philosophy, I wanted to teach about Jesus," he says. It was Mary Ellen who told him, "Keep praying. Something else will surely come along." That *something else* appeared in the form of an invitation from St. Joseph College to teach theology and Scripture to individuals training to become lay church leaders. Don adds, "I'm learning things about Scripture I'd never had the opportunity to study before."

Several weeks later, they received a request from the local minimum-security prison. Would they be willing to meet once a week with prisoners who want to study the Bible? Don tells us that St. Gaspar spent the first years of his priestly ministry in an Italian prison. "We don't preach," Don wants to make clear, "but we sit in a circle with the inmates, taking turns thoughtfully reading a passage from Scripture, reflecting quietly, then sharing with one another whatever strikes us about the words."

They both talk about what attracted them to the Missionaries of the Precious Blood. "Christ's reconciliation by peaceful means was what resonated with me in my teachings," says Don, "especially my connection to the Catholic Worker Movement and the International Peace Bureau." For Mary Ellen, who had endured the pain of losing her first husband, compassion for the suffering of others is the gift she treasures most from the Precious Blood tradition. "When you lose a spouse or a child, you reexamine your life," she says. Her compassion is clear in her stories of Africa: the mothers forced to watch their children starve because of a drought, the sick dying without medical help, the uneducated hungry for knowledge.

Until they became companions, Don and Mary Ellen hadn't fully understood the vision and gifts of St. Gaspar, which drive the mission of the Society. "The Precious Blood spirituality and all that St. Gaspar stood for is now the center of our life," says Mary Ellen. Receiving the wine – the blood of Christ – at Mass has taken on a deeper meaning for both of them. Mary Ellen explains: "When you accept the wine, you say *Yes* to accepting suffering, to being compassionate toward the suffering of others, to being open to the invitation of Jesus as a source of peace in the world." Don adds that becoming a companion has heightened his search for ways to resolve conflict nonviolently, for ways of bringing people together. His Scripture study has been enlightened by his connection to the Precious Blood spirituality. "Participating in Eucharist should change us," says Don. "We are nourished so that we can feed the hunger of the world, as Jesus did, spiritually as well as in body.

Don and Mary Ellen are missionaries. "We're spreading the spirit of St. Gaspar wherever we're called," they say, from the people of Tanzania, five thousand miles away, to the prisoners of Indiana, five minutes from home.

Seven

Audrey Bagnowski

Associate of the Sisters of St. Francis

Audrey Bagnowski with her sister

How it improves people for us when we begin to love them.
David Grayson

Like most of us, Audrey Bagnowski carries vivid memories – some of them heart-warming, some of them painful.

"I remember my dad carrying me – at age five or six – on his shoulders into church during a rainstorm. What an introduction to God the Father by my father! I remember my mother reading stories to me about Jesus and how much He loved me."

But Audrey can also recall herself as a lonely thirteen-year-old, grieving over the sudden death of her father. She remembers how the Sisters of St. Francis, her teachers at St. Ladislaus High School, in a suburb outside Detroit, Michigan, supported her and became part of her extended family. The sisters lived what Audrey has come to call "The Franciscan Walk," a path this counselor for mentally and physically handicapped individuals now sees as her own way of life.

"The sisters, knowing my Dad had just died, picked up what he could no longer do," she recalls. "They encouraged my intellect, my love for writing and theater, my creativity and risk-taking." The sisters laid the groundwork for a much later call to partnership as an associate with their community. "My life over the years," she says, "has evolved into living the Prayer of St. Francis."

Audrey recalls one connection with the sisters during eleventh grade that had an impact on her. It was 1968, and Sister Yvonne had taken a group of students, including Audrey, to a Poor Peoples' March, where they demonstrated for greater government assistance for the poor, particularly for Black people. "While marching, we got our picture taken, and it was published in *Michigan Catholic*, the diocesan newspaper." Audrey's neighbors took offense at her participation in the march, but her mother defended her actions. "She told the neighbors that she was proud of me for standing up for what I believed in, that you have to respect all people, no matter their color." But the country, and especially Detroit, was torn by racial tension at this time, and there was an escalating level of fear and misunderstanding. Audrey's family was shocked to find eggs thrown at their house and damage to their car and property. "Sister Yvonne's courage and leadership helped us get through it, helped us keep faith," Audrey recalls.

Actually, the seeds for Audrey's connection to the Sisters of St. Francis had been planted much earlier, since her aunt, Sister Cornelia, was a member of the community. "My aunt was a very strong influence and role model for me," she explains, "the first person in our family to receive her Master's Degree." Audrey became the second. For most of her childhood, Audrey, her parents, and her sister Judy enjoyed monthly visits with Sister Cornelia, getting to know the other sisters in the community along the way.

"What stood out about the sisters was their down-to-earth approach to life," she says. "There was always a joy and peace and aliveness that shone through." And their concern for poor and homeless people, especially women and children, led her to choose a career dedicated to the less fortunate.

Audrey's call to be an associate of the Sisters of St. Francis came just months after her beloved aunt, Sister Cornelia, had died of a heart attack. Sister Felice Gorny befriended her during her grief and eventually invited her to consider connecting more closely to the community. She became an associate in 1986, but had to drop out for a few years due to her lack of transportation. In April of 1995, Audrey renewed her association.

"The associates meet four times a year for a half day and for an annual weekend retreat," she says. Audrey and Sister Felice meet monthly to talk about what is going on in their lives, how God is leading and guiding them. As an added outreach of her journey, Audrey enjoys sharing her spiritual life with Sister Brenda Rose, a Sister of St. Francis, who acts as her spiritual director. "This has been a catalyst for growth," she says. "We review where I am spiritually, looking for ways to continue my journey toward forgiveness, and to move forward in expectant faith."

"My contacts with the sisters have given me the courage to change into the person God is calling me to be. To know that I am supported in love and prayer in this way makes the unbearable bearable."

The Franciscan Walk for Audrey has been a journey of forgiveness – of others, of herself. The night before her father died, Audrey remembers having had an argument with him, and afterwards refusing him her customary goodnight kiss. "I blamed myself for his death because of our argument and felt guilty for years." Just recently, through membership in a faith-sharing group, she was able to heal the hurt, remembering all the times they had kissed goodnight. "By forgiving myself I gained the freedom to walk in the positive, wishing healing thoughts for myself, my family, my friends. By pardoning myself and my father, I experienced God's forgiveness within."

These days, Audrey strums her guitar as a music minister at her church's evening worship, but she remembers the years she buried her talent and her guitar. As she approaches middle age, she can still recall the anger and pain she felt at age eighteen when her parish priest refused to let her become a lector and eucharistic minister at Mass. She remembers the years she harbored the anger, migrating to other parishes and eventually leaving the Church for a time.

Reflecting on the prayer of St. Francis, especially the words, *Where there is injury, pardon,* Audrey felt called to seek the sacrament of Penance at a nearby church. "I wanted to go to confession. I wanted to forgive the priest who had denied me the opportunity to be a lector and eucharistic minister for my parish," a hurt and anger she had carried in her heart for nearly thirty years. "I gave that whole instance to the Lord. I forgave the priest." At that moment she felt the power of love and pardon. "Since then I have felt at peace with the Church."

As she journeys the Franciscan Walk, Audrey finds constant guidance and inspiration in St. Francis' prayer. The words, *Let me sow love,* have become her motto as a professional counselor. After college, she followed Sister Yvonne's inspiration and began working as a relocation social worker in the most poverty-stricken areas of Detroit. "I learned I had to be steeped in prayer in order to counteract the negativity and heartbreak I saw every day," she says. Audrey's journey in social work has led her to a position as a vocational rehabilitation counselor for the State of Michigan Department of Career Development. Sixty percent of her clients have severe mental conditions. "I help the jobless, those with low self-esteem, those who've struggled with suicide and hopelessness," she says. "I feel empathy for those who have not been loved. More and more I see how the conditions my clients have are frequently the result of a lack of love."

Audrey has presented seminars and spoken nationally on the need for accommodations in the workplace for people with emotional and physical disabilities. She sees her work as the "ultimate call of a peacemaker." In 1998 she was one of fourteen professional counselors in Michigan to be honored as Counselor of the Year. She attributes her success to "living in a carefree Franciscan state of mind," explaining that it involves integration of mind, heart, body and soul. "The Sisters of St. Francis," she adds, "have been an important part of that integration. They have led by their example."

As if to show the clients she serves that physical handicaps need not limit them, Audrey shares another memory of herself – a woman in a lifelong struggle with asthma. She has suffered two respiratory arrests, with close to twenty rushed trips to the emergency room – not coincidentally, at a Franciscan hospital. During both respiratory arrests, Audrey remembers feeling the prayers of the sisters, and she was able to return to work within ten days. Eventually, through a series of tests, doctors identified certain food additives as the contributing factors in shutting down Audrey's lungs, and since that time, she has been able to manage her asthma symptoms.

"My sufferings with asthma helped me realize that I am not in control – that I need to trust that God is leading me." People with her level of severity are rarely able to hold a job, but Audrey has done just that for more than twenty-five years. "As I have become stronger and go deeper on my walk with God, I feel God is healing the asthma," she says. "I have been challenged to let go of this sickness." She explains that, when a person lives with a chronic illness, it becomes an acute part of the self, because one has to deal with it on a daily basis. "I had to be willing to see myself as a healthy woman. I've had to disown the sickness as St. Francis disowned his ties with the world, so that God could do His work."

As an associate, Audrey sees herself as answering a call to be a Franciscan. "This is a call to full personhood, with freedom to be a missionary of sorts – right here as I live my life." And as she continues to heal the painful memories, she says she is starting to "get the hang of what the Gospel is all about…. God has helped me to reduce my attachment to things, in order to enrich and deepen my ministries within the Franciscan Walk…to laugh at myself, to fall in love all over again with God, with oneself, with the world."

Eight

Guy Mazzola

Associate of the Congregation of the Incarnate Word and Blessed Sacrament

Then God put out his hand and touched my mouth and said to me: "Now I have put my words in your mouth." Jeremiah 1:9

*I*t came as the result of a promise. In the early 1970s, Guy Mazzola and his wife had lost a baby during pregnancy. In the following months, Guy read a book about Mother Jeanne Chezard de Matel, foundress of the Congregation of the Incarnate Word and Blessed Sacrament. "Her life and works fascinated me," he says, "and a spiritual bond developed." He made an agreement with the holy woman. "I promised Mother Jeanne that, if she interceded and our next child arrived safely, I would do whatever she wanted whenever she directed me."

On June 16, 1976, a healthy daughter was born. "I thought of my promise often," Guy says, "but received nothing I could identify as a *sign*." Then in 1979, Sister Jean Marie Guokas, a former teacher of Guy's wife and friend to the family, asked him to become a member of the first Advisory Board of Incarnate

Word Academy, the primary ministry of the sisters in Houston, Texas. As a busy professional, he had reasons to decline the invitation, but not wanting to disappoint his friend, he accepted. Later he began regretting the decision, finding a list of excuses for not serving on the board.

One day as he was driving home, he received what he calls "a very clear message" that his service on the Advisory Board was the fulfillment of his promise to Mother Jeanne de Matel. "As I began to fulfill my promise," he says, "I fell in love – in love with the foundress' charism, philosophy, spirituality, way of life." He couldn't explain what was happening to him. "The farther I went, the farther I needed to go. Mother Jeanne's spirit was infectious."

Guy found himself reading all he could about Mother Jeanne, referring to her as *Our Foundress*. He found himself praying to her regularly, sometimes several times a day. "A true dialogue had begun," he says, "but one that I did not understand."

Guy began to experience a feeling that something was missing in his life, although he could not identify it. He began attending daily Mass, thinking this might be the solution to his feeling of emptiness. As the feelings recurred, he consulted with his parish priest, a Dominican, who recommended he join the Dominican Third Order. "I had no call to become a Dominican, and I found a number of excuses not to join," he says.

Attempting to deal with the "missing feelings," he sought the advice of Sister Jean Marie, who taught him to recite the Prayers of the Hours – the official prayer of the Church. This helped for a brief time, but the feelings persisted. During this period of unrest, the Congregation of the Incarnate Word had been discussing the status of associate membership, although the community had not made a decision whether to accept or offer such status to lay people. Guy knew nothing about the discussions or association.

For Guy, it was a period of great struggle. "Here I was a married Roman Catholic man with a family, yet I was experiencing a *calling*...but a calling to what?" Other than the status of volunteer, Guy felt there was no place for him in the Church he loved. Still a member of the Advisory Board of Incarnate Word Academy, he had indeed become associated with a group of sisters whose philosophy, lifestyle, and ministry was becoming part of his very being. "Family and close friends saw a change in me," he recalls. "Some expressed approval, others were not so understanding. Feelings of misplacement and *Why me, Lord?* came regularly."

During 1985, Guy often met with Sister Jean Marie, who had been elected Superior General of the community. During one visit, Guy began to tell her about his feelings and about his unwillingness to join the Dominican Third Order. "Just wait," Sister Jean Marie told him. "Our community is talking about association. Just wait!" Guy was not familiar with association, but he did as she asked.

It was nearly five years later before Sister Jean Marie again addressed the issue of association with Guy, explaining the associate status, which had been a vital part of the Incarnate Word community during the life of the foundress. Sister Jean Marie asked Guy to serve on the committee that would investigate re-instating associate membership. She wanted him to make a recommendation to the Council. The first meeting on March 24, 1990, was the beginning, says Guy, "of a journey that would change my life forever."

That committee recommended that the Council of the Incarnate Word community adopt the status of associate membership. Guy was asked to represent the committee and address the sisters in a general meeting. It was known that various members of the community had different levels of opinions and had expressed many concerns. An attorney by education, Guy had appeared before various judicial officials from federal judges to hearing officers. "But nothing in my professional life could compare with this assignment," he recalls. While it was a privilege to address the community, he also felt the responsibility, since the community would vote after hearing his address.

Guy prepared an outline, feeling that delivering a written speech would not be fitting. "In the middle of the talk, I found myself using plural possessive phrases concerning the community: *our charism, our Foundress, our order.*" Mentally he thought, "Oh God, I've blown it! Surely the sisters will question this level of familiarity." After the speech he nervously paced the hall and prayed to the foundress to forgive his failure.

After a brief time, one of the sisters found him in the hallway and handed him a card with the picture of Mother Jeanne. "It passed," she told him. "They're for it! Your use of *our* is what won them over." Guy was overjoyed. The study was over and the work of establishing association had begun.

The community appointed a spiritual director for associates, Sister Anastasia, and invited people to consider joining. Guy was one of the first to apply. A committee comprised of sisters and pre-associates was formed to develop a structured formation process, along with a plan for spiritual development, and a schedule of monthly meetings for fellowship and prayer with vowed members of the community.

Associate status is now well developed in the Incarnate Word community, with associates working in community ministries such as parish work, teaching, and care for the homebound. "The most gratifying stage of the development," says Guy, "is to see the activity not only within the Church, but also in the civic community, where our associates carry the charism and are living examples of Incarnation spirituality – living in the world as an extension of the Word of God." The associates have studied and adopted the charism. "To see these sister and brother associates find their place in the religious order," says Guy, "and to become daughters and sons of our Foundress, is a joy shared by both vowed and associate members alike."

As for the feelings that had nagged him, the feelings that he was missing something in his life – they stopped. The cure? "Community. Once I felt that I was part of the order, all became whole," he says. "My call to serve became clear." He remembers his first community ceremony. Looking up at a stained-glass image of Jesus, the Incarnate Word, centered in the Convent chapel, he felt he finally belonged. "My purpose was now defined," he explains. "I was to be an associate and work with the community in ministries – and in its associate program." For Guy Mazzola, that was the moment he discovered his call, his place in the Church.

Nine

Elizabeth Browne

Partner of the Passionist Fathers

*My grace is sufficient for you, for power is made perfect in
weakness.* 2 Corinthians 12:9

"Let me tell you how he got his name," says Elizabeth
Browne about her guide dog. This Doctor of Philosophy and
teacher of English literature and theology at Loyola University,
Chicago, loves a good story. Elizabeth replays the day she was
forced to retire her old guide dog after nine years. Feeling guilty
and sad at the loss, she had approached the Guide Dog School to
begin the process of choosing a new dog.

Because Elizabeth was in an unfamiliar setting, she
recalls, "I ran smack into a door, causing a nosebleed and a cut
over my eye. I sank into the nearest chair, tears and blood trailing
down my face." Seconds later, a large dog nosed his way toward
her, lay his chin in her lap, and then began licking the blood and
tears from her face. "I said, *That's my dog!* and I named him after
the saint who loved lepers enough to lick their sores."

Damian of Molokai, her two-year-old golden retriever, bounces up from his *down* position, hoping to be petted. Elizabeth, a tiny woman with a wide smile across high cheekbones, fusses at her honey-colored companion. "He's still a puppy," she excuses his friskiness.

For Elizabeth, losing her sight was an accident, but receiving the gift of faith was not. She remembers special moments from her childhood when she sensed there was a God who loved her simply for herself. She was the youngest child of Italian immigrant parents who worked separate shifts to make ends meet.

"Ma, are we Catholic?" she asked when she was seven. "Of course we're Catholic, we're Italian," answered her mother, a woman burdened with an epileptic son, a woman who worked second shift and didn't have time to see that her four children went to church.

"But Ma," Elizabeth pleaded, "all my friends in the Catholic school are making their First Communion. If I'm a Catholic, I want to make mine too."

"OK," her mother answered, "go ahead."

Elizabeth remembers how special her First Communion Day was. The dress and veil weren't fancy and the prayer book was plain, but she was filled with happiness receiving Jesus. "I remember so clearly after Mass," she says, "coming out of Church and watching as the other girls and boys were hugged by their parents and all their relatives." Then she spotted her older brother across the street in a scruffy shirt and pants. "C'mon Sis," he said, "I'm here to walk you home." Alone and aware of her lack of a celebration, she had every right to feel unhappy. "But I wasn't. I remember feeling that this was an important moment."

Walking home with her brother, her white stockings drooping (she had dressed herself), a woman crossed the street to congratulate her. "She looked me over, took out two quarters from her pocketbook, hoisted up my stockings and twisted a coin in each hem to hold them up." She refers to that moment as a "glimpse of God's compassion." From that day, she began to attend Mass every Sunday, although the rest of her family did not.

When she was nine, Elizabeth was at a roller-skating party where she ended up at the bottom of a pileup, someone's skates crashing into her skull. Afraid to trouble her parents, she masked the headaches that followed, but eventually her double vision and fading sight were discovered. A series of remedies and unsuccessful surgery led to permanent blindness.

After her release from the hospital, she expected to resume her normal life of play, music, learning, and drawing. Instead, exclusion was what she experienced. Even the neighborhood children who had once been her playmates threw stones at her when she approached them, fearing they would "catch" her blindness. She was placed in a special school for the blind and demoted to first grade because she could not read Braille. The blind children were locked in their classroom during recess. One day a substitute teacher recognized Elizabeth's intelligence and arranged for her to attend a regular public school at the appropriate grade level. It was the beginning of her liberation – a journey toward opening others' eyes to a suffering population.

Her family's financial limitations and her blindness kept her in public school, but her strong faith led her to seek the sacrament of Confirmation. While preparing for Confirmation, the Bishop visited her and other Catholic students in the neighborhood public school. "What can I do for you?" he asked. Elizabeth did not hesitate. "I want to go to the Catholic high school like everyone in my neighborhood," she told him. "It shall be done," the Bishop responded, and she received a scholarship to Loretto High School. The Sisters of Loretto were less than enthusiastic about admitting a blind girl. "They didn't really want to accept me," Elizabeth chuckles, "but after my first year, they were beating the bushes to find other girls with handicaps!"

After high school, a scholarship to Rosary College followed. Her faith blossomed, and during her first year of college she began to believe she was being called to deepen her spirituality. In the 1950s, young women drawn to a deeper spiritual life had only one choice: the convent. Elizabeth found herself an outcast again, when one order of nuns after another refused her. Finally, a contemplative order of Dominican sisters said yes, and she spent a year with them. "I loved every minute of it," she says, "and the sisters loved me. But something told me that I was meant to live in the world."

She returned to Rosary College – and to a young man named Ed Browne, whom she had dated during her freshman year. She shows us her engagement ring – a pearl in a gold setting – adding, "Ed called me a pearl of great price." Her smile turns serious. "He never seemed to notice my blindness. He fell in love with *me*, not a blind woman. In fact," she gears up for another story, "after our meeting at a college mixer, he called me for a date. When I told him I was testing Christmas tree lights, he wasn't sure he had the right girl." Engaged on Christmas Day, 1953, Elizabeth and Ed shared a desire for a richer spiritual life. During this pre-Vatican II period, both got involved in the Christian Family Movement, as they raised their two girls and three boys. Over the years, they have guided their children toward service to the less fortunate.

Although Elizabeth was not closely acquainted with the Passionist community during her early years, her hunger for the spiritual and her experience as a blind person formed the groundwork for her role as a Passionist Partner. She traces her first contact with the community to Father Bennett, a Passionist priest she had met while a student at Rosary College. "He was a humble man," she says, "and he always had time to talk with me. Every Wednesday we'd visit and go for a walk, then have lunch in the cafeteria. He'd rave about the pork chops," she recalls, "but he'd order a cheese sandwich." It was then she realized the Passionist custom of abstaining from meat on Wednesdays and Fridays to commemorate Christ's Passion.

Later, when she was teaching English at St. Xavier College in Chicago, Father Donald Senior, a Passionist priest who was president of the Catholic Theological Union (CTU) in Chicago, invited her to be part of a panel at CTU. It was the 1980s and the United Nations had declared it the Decade of the Disabled. "At first I asked: *Why me? I'm not disabled!* But I'm glad I went, because after that Father Don invited me to attend one of his theology classes at CTU." There, she met the Passionist writer and theologian Carroll Stuhlmueller, and a friendship formed. "I felt at home with them," she says, "and I liked their philosophy. I liked the fact that they identify so closely with people suffering in the world today."

At first, Elizabeth balked at the Old Testament theology classes she took at CTU. "I kept noticing how people with disabilities were portrayed as outcasts," she explains, "and I thought: *I don't much like this God of the Old Testament.*" But she was encouraged to keep studying, and her perseverance led to the formulation of her own *Theology of the Outcast,* a theme she has woven into a collection of her life stories. One of those stories involves Father Ken O'Malley, a Passionist priest who worked with her in the mid-1990s as a mentor and support person to lay missioners – student volunteers who live and work for a year in Chicago's inner city. Teaming with Father Ken, she met once a week with volunteers, offering advice, prayer and reflection, and support in their ministry. "Father Ken didn't seem to notice I was a blind person," she marvels. "We trounced through some pretty rough places, even challenged drug dealers who were harassing our volunteers," she laughs. Ken O'Malley never once said, "Oh, Elizabeth's blind. She can't do that." Because the Passionists are so in touch with Christ's suffering, she explains, they have a special sensitivity to human pain.

The invitation to become a Partner with the Passionists seemed a natural for Elizabeth. "You're already working with us," Father Don Senior said, referring to Elizabeth's role in support of Passionist lay volunteers, "and you're here all the time teaching and working on your dissertation [*The Disabled Disciple,* which won the 1998 Catholic Press Award], so why don't you become one of us?" During a year of formation with Father Don and other Passionist friends, Elizabeth and her husband Ed prepared together for their formal commitment. "I missed a few Saturday Days of Recollection because I teach," she says, "so I wondered if I was ready." The Passionist community told her, "We all think you're ready, and we want you to join us!"

The Passionist philosophy – transforming suffering and pain in your everyday life into something positive – was what bolstered Elizabeth during difficult times in her career as a teacher. "Suffering, unrelated to Christ's Passion," she says, "is meaningless. If you're dealt hardships, make something of it."

When, at age eleven, she had told her first teacher in the blind school that she wanted to be a teacher, he, also blind, had answered, "Forget about teaching sighted people. You'll never be able to do it." Her faith told her differently. "I'm me. Not a blind person. At least that's how I chose to view it." She remembers the teaching jobs she was refused because of her blindness. Then she smiles as she recalls the joy of being hired as a teacher at Mundelein College based on her resume, *sight unseen.*

For Elizabeth, Partnership involves continuing her ministry to the outcast, focusing on Christ's Passion in today's world, so that people will be accepted for their true worth. "My gift is to be a human being witnessing to Christ's Passion in the world," she says, "and that fits with the Passionist message very well." Four times a year she and other Partners gather to study, pray, share and deepen their bonds. Passionist Partners also volunteer to fast between meals and abstain from meat on Wednesdays and Fridays, remembering in a concrete way the suffering in the world. And Elizabeth and her husband have promised to continue to incorporate prayer into their daily life.

Her golden retriever Damian sits up suddenly, indicating it's time to sniff around the campus and check out the bushes on this rainy April Sunday. She pats his soft head, saying, "Damian goes to daily Mass with us." The gentle dog gives his large tail a sweep, and Elizabeth smiles again. "I guess you could say Damian is a Passionist Partner, too!"

Ten

Terry Ulery

Companion of the Missionaries of the Precious Blood

It is not the great accomplishments done in one's life, but the little accomplishments done with great love of God.
                                                    Mother Teresa of Calcutta.

*T*he two-story yellow-brick rowhouses are neat and orderly. They line a downtown street in a transitional neighborhood of Cleveland that still appears down on its luck. It's mealtime at Malachi House, a home for the dying poor in Cleveland, Ohio, and residents, staff, and volunteers are enjoying home-cooked lasagna around the dining room table.

There is chatter and laughter, in spite of the telltale signs of terminal illness. One person slumps in a wheelchair, eyes blank with pain. Others bustle around, their bald heads the only sign of their struggle against disease. None of them is a stranger to Terry Ulery.

"Every person in this house has a story – one more heartbreaking than the other," says Terry, a redheaded woman with searching green eyes. She remembers a man whose face

59

was so disfigured with cancer that he would not leave his small apartment to get treatment. One evening, in desperation, his daughter came to Malachi House. Terry, then Executive Director, jumped in her van and followed the woman home. "It was the expression of acceptance on my face when I removed his bandages that convinced him to come to Malachi House that very night," she says. "I told him not to worry. I'd seen a lot worse."

And that was true. A licensed practical nurse who ministers to the sick and dying, Terry had not been able to save her younger brother from the devastation of cancer at age thirty. He left a grieving wife with four children, ages six weeks to seven years. Two years later, cancer began to consume Terry's mother. And while she was nursing her mother at home, Terry's husband was diagnosed with cancer. Aggressive treatment left him unable to work for more than three years. Terry became not only the main caregiver but also the sole breadwinner for their family of four children.

Terry's husband was on the road to a full recovery when she was hospitalized with an abdominal tumor. She was advised to prepare for aggressive chemotherapy by building up her health. She followed the doctor's advice. At the same time, she also began to build up her spiritual health. A year before, in 1981, she had made a weekend retreat while caring for her husband. "I experienced God living in each and every human being. It was truly an awakening, where I actually felt touched by God," she recalls. This led her to join a prayer group at her Cleveland parish, Our Lady of Good Counsel, run by the Missionaries of the Precious Blood (C.PP.S), and to seek spiritual direction from one of the fathers.

While waiting for her own test results, she placed herself in God's hands and in the hands of those who ministered to her from her church and prayer group. When she went for further tests, she and her doctor were amazed to find the tumor had disappeared. She was given a clean bill of health.

"I felt we had experienced several miracles over the years, but this one was different," she says. Terry saw it as a call from God that had to be answered. With the help of her spiritual director, Father Jim, C.PP.S., and the blessing of her husband, she decided she would give her nursing skills to the poor – free of charge – for an unspecified period of time. She prayed to God for guidance.

The answer came one week later. She found her daughter in tears about a classmate whose father was dying of cancer. The child's mother was ill with a heart problem, and there were seven children and a grandchild, all under eighteen, living in a roach-infested house, just a few streets from Terry's home. "Tell them I'll come to see them tomorrow," she told her daughter. "I was shocked at the poverty – no food in the refrigerator, no sheets on the bed, and most of the children sleeping on the floor." Neighbors had labeled the children "unruly." *This is a well-kept neighborhood,* Terry thought. *How could we not have noticed or tried to help this family in their crisis?*

Terry promised the man, who had been sleeping in a chair, that she would get him a hospital bed. "I had no idea where I was going to find one," she laughs. But her call to the Cancer Society brought a bed the next day. The St. Vincent de Paul Society in her parish provided food, and Terry and her husband donated dairy products. The father ended his days with dignity in a Catholic nursing home – the same one that had welcomed her mother during the final weeks when Terry and her twin sister, Josie, could no longer care for her at home. Her daughter's friend told her mother, "See Mom, I told you Mrs. Ulery's just like Santa Claus!" Terry had found her ministry – working with dying poor people.

Within days, she got word of another family in need. Through various parishes in neighboring areas, referrals began pouring in. Along with two other members of her parish prayer group, and with the spiritual support of the parish priests, she went into the homes of the dying to care for them. Then, in 1989, she felt guided to volunteer at Malachi House, a new non-profit home for Cleveland's dying poor people. The unique, faith-based home accepts no payment; indigence and terminal illness are the only criteria for admission. Before long she became the home's Volunteer Coordinator, then Executive Director.

Terry's relationship with the Precious Blood fathers in her parish began to grow and deepen as she ministered to the dying poor at Malachi House. She remembers the day she barged in on the newly appointed priest in her parish, following the death of a resident, a 42-year-old mother of two young children. The woman had escaped an abusive husband addicted to drugs, and her final request was that Terry find a suitable home for her children. "Don't stop me," Terry told the priest. "I've got to let it out." Then she says, "I just cried and cried." Along with the comfort of a listening ear, the priest offered her a book of meditations.

A few weeks later, she noticed one of the volunteers at Malachi House using the same book. "Paul (the volunteer) could see that I needed support," she recalls. "He was a companion of the Precious Blood, and he offered to meet with me to pray." Their once-a-month meetings led to Terry's year of discernment before deciding to become a companion. Her covenant with the Precious Blood community includes support of the community, service to those who are suffering, and daily prayer. "The prayer, for me, is a must," she insists. "Without time with the Lord, I can't do anything else."

Companions of the Precious Blood share in the spiritual life of the community through formal and informal prayer, and in small prayer groups. Terry comes together in prayer with about fifteen companions in the Cleveland area. "We're very close. I can call any one of them any time for support. No appointment needed. That, to me, is very special." In fact, many of the Precious Blood Companions have joined Terry in her ministry as volunteers at Malachi House.

Community feast day celebrations and days of prayer keep her connected to the Precious Blood community. "It took a lot of prayers to get to where I am in this ministry," she says. "Still, when the demands at Malachi House become overwhelming, meeting the needs of the residents often becomes my prayer."

Terry can trace her call to serve poor people to when she was fourteen. She joined the Franciscan Sisters as an aspirant, but by sixteen, she knew that way of life was not for her. "I wanted to be a nun and a nurse," she says, "but I know now that God needed me more as a nurse and a mother." Yet she believes the desire she had as a fourteen-year-old is being fulfilled as a companion. "I can be in a community and still do the nursing ministry I've always loved." Terry's husband and their children, all grown, are supportive of her association with the Precious Blood community. "My husband is growing with me," she says, "and our kids have found their own ways to express their spirituality. We're together as a team!"

The family team expanded in 1993 when Terry's twin sister, Josie, joined the staff at Malachi House as a nurse. A few years later, they traded positions, Josie becoming Executive Director, so that Terry could devote more time to resident care. But while Josie loves her work with dying poor people, she does not feel the same call to become a companion.

In Terry's earliest years as a nurse, she was constantly guided to terminally ill patients. She tells the story of an eighteen-year-old girl in danger of dying who was near panic. "I gave her a little cross I had carried in my pocket since my days in the convent," she says, "and we prayed together." The next morning the girl told her she had never slept more peacefully. "I told her to keep the cross." A day later, Terry was saddened to learn the girl had died, yet she also experienced a sense of peace. "I knew I had reached somebody."

Other nurses began asking her to sit with dying patients. "God slowly took my anxiety away, so that I felt comfortable with them." She remembers thinking, "What a blessing to be with someone actively dying...to be able to help them approach this moment without fear."

Her journey to Malachi House involved anger, depression, and denial. "I felt God was really nailing me. I was not happy with God, and I had to pass through all those steps of death and dying before I could move into acceptance." It was the Precious Blood fathers at her parish, she says, who walked with her and who continue to draw her to love and compassion.

"When my brother died, I started focusing on the terminally ill," she remembers, but it began in anger. "I was furious that God would take my brother and spare the poor bums on the street." She closes her eyes and shakes her head. Then her face lights with a wry smile. "And yet today, that's exactly what I'm doing – taking care of those bums. Now I see them as very special people."

Eleven

Tim Simmons

Associate of the Sisters of Mercy

Kristin and Tim Simmons

I thought about being a priest. I prayed about it. But I know that is not what I am being called to do. Still, I am being called – to something spiritual, something active. It's exciting to me, because I think that, in association, I've found it. This is where I need to be –connected. That's the call. And I'm trying to answer it.   *Tim Simmons, Mercy Associate*

*H*e talks fast, his eyes wide open, hands waving. One minute he is laughing, his angular face broad with a smile, as he mentions his marriage partner, his promising future. The next minute, his dark eyes narrow in serious thought. At twenty-six, Tim Simmons remembers the troubled kid he was in high school, due to what he describes as *family problems*. It was his teachers who helped him through those difficult years. "I was drawn to teaching," he adds, "because I wanted to go back into a classroom and do for others what my teachers had done for me."

At twenty-three, Tim Simmons graduated from college in his hometown of Philadelphia with an education degree and a year of student teaching under his belt. But openings in the suburban schools where he applied were few, and the jobs went to more experienced teachers. At a volunteer fair, he picked up a

65

brochure about Mercy Volunteer Corps and checked it out. Before he knew it, he had decided to give the next year as a volunteer. "I liked the sites they offered in the American West, and I figured I might as well go where teachers are needed."

His reasons for volunteering seemed more practical than heroic at the time. There were no jobs teaching English in suburban Philly, but there was a teaching job in a place he loved – the American Southwest. He also wanted to see if he was up to the challenge.

Simple living. These two words sum up one of the most important lessons Tim learned as a volunteer teacher with Mercy Volunteer Corps, sponsored by the Sisters of Mercy of the Americas. Living in community at St. Michael School on a Navajo Reservation in Arizona, he was free of worries about material things. Without all the distractions of making a living, he could devote his full attention to the kids he taught, to his own spiritual life, and to building community with the people who lived with him.

When the first year was over, he signed up for another. "I could not get over how much it challenged me, touched me. I am amazed how much I still draw on that experience every day. It's affected *everything*: the way I teach, the way I live my life, the way I pray, the way I see the world." Tim adds with a grin that, thanks to Mercy Volunteer Corps, he met Kristin Salloom, also a Mercy volunteer at St Michael's in Arizona, who has become his wife.

After his two years on the Navajo reservation, Tim returned to Philadelphia to pursue his career as a high school English teacher. During his time in Arizona, his parents had sold the family home and downsized, so his first challenge came in finding his own apartment. Then came the expenses and the bills for rent, utilities, credit cards, insurance. Not feeling ready to handle inner-city teaching, he settled for a sixth-grade math job in an outlying suburb. Before long he began dreading the traffic and the long commute. "After the volunteer thing," he recalls, "it was a smack in the face. As a volunteer, I had been able to forget about all that stuff. Now I was on my own, and I felt like I was barely keeping my head above water. I really missed the support of a community."

After a full year of feeling isolated and overwhelmed, Tim

was tempted to call St. Michael's in Arizona and say, "I'm coming back!" Instead he phoned Sister Eileen Campbell, Executive Director of Mercy Volunteer Corps. She invited him to become part of the Mercy Volunteer Corps team during the summers, helping to recruit and train new volunteers. "I was so glad," Tim says. "It gave me a way to stay connected to Mercy and the spirit of community I'd grown to love."

"Then out of the blue," he says, "just as I was preparing to go back to my sixth-grade math job, I was offered a teaching position at Gwynedd-Mercy High School!" The school, on the same campus with the college and the volunteer office, was in need of a sophomore English teacher. "I didn't hesitate," he says. "I saw this as a way to deepen my connection with the whole Mercy family."

Tim says he still needed guidance balancing his desire for simple living with managing a budget, paying bills, and living the hectic life of a high-school teacher. He turned to the Sisters of Mercy he had come to appreciate through Mercy Volunteer Corps and at Gwynedd-Mercy High School. "At one time, I had thought the only way I could recapture the simple living thing was to move back to Arizona. Just pack up my car and go back and say that this fast-paced lifestyle was not for me," he remembers. "But I was wrong. This is my life now, and I like what I do." He laughs as he admits he even likes the convenience of his credit cards. "But it has to be reconciled with what I discovered about myself in Arizona…that I need community, that my work needs to be of service to others."

The kinship between Mercy volunteers is special, and in Tim and Kristin's case, it became the basis for a much deeper relationship. "We were both searching for a life where we could experience a sense of community, and where we could be of service and develop spiritually," Tim explains, "and those aspects – the components of Mercy Volunteer Corps – were also there in association."

Connecting with the Mercy community as an associate seemed a natural next step, especially since Kristin – on her own – had also felt drawn to become a Mercy associate. The two made their first covenant with the sisters on the feast of Our Lady of Mercy, September 24, 1999. "Still, it was a hard decision for me,"

Tim says. "During the year of associate orientation, I went back and forth. It's a big commitment." Then he breaks into his laugh again. "Actually the truth is, I got a little nervous every time I thought about standing up in front of all my grade-school teachers at the covenant ceremony!"

Tim was educated by Sisters of Mercy in grade school, and attended a Jesuit high school and college. But it wasn't until he returned to a Mercy school as a teacher that, he says, "It clicked that I was being led toward the idea of membership through association. It was the hospitality of the sisters that really called to me."

A few months before making their covenant, he and Kristin stood before the whole community of sisters and associates of Merion, Pennsylvania, as they and other pre-associates were introduced. "I looked out on those faces," he says, "wondering how they'd feel about accepting a young man into their community." He thought of the trouble he must have caused some of those very sisters who knew him in grade school. "I've sometimes experienced older people who discount my ideas because of my youth. But that didn't happen with the Mercys. From the start, I have felt respected by these wise women."

"It's part of the Mercy charism," he explains. "I think it's really Christian, the way the Mercys make everyone feel so welcome. It's unique. I really like that. It's the way I want to be towards others.

"Being a part of the Mercy community has been good for me," he says. He recalls his growth as a teacher in Arizona. He has deepened his prayer life through the training and workshops he's given to new Mercy Corps volunteers. "Being a part of the Mercy community has made me a better teacher," he explains, "because the sisters and other associates challenge me to share my gifts with my students."

Partnership with the Sisters of Mercy, an Institute with ministries around the world, also appeals to Tim. "I feel like I'm part of a bigger picture." His experience with Mercy Volunteer Corps awakened him to other cultures and the needs of poor people. With his students, he continues to explore volunteer opportunities. "I'm hoping that, through association, I can stay close to the poor in a prayerful context," he says. "Joined with the sisters and other associates, I can make that spiritual connection."

Tim Simmons doesn't have a fortune, but he admits he's been lucky, and he wants to do something about it. He's more aware of ways to bring about change for others less fortunate, especially in downtown Philadelphia. With the support of the Sisters of Mercy, he's determined to do something. "Or else I've got to shut up," he laughs. "And I don't see that happening!"

Twelve
Suzanne Kathman
Associate of the Sisters of Mercy

Sue Kathman with an elderly client

*As a Mercy associate, I became immersed in the community.
I put my arms completely around the community, and I felt
the community put its arms completely around me.*
Sue Kathman

Sue Kathman was a successful thirty-something, estranged from the Catholic faith that had been her heritage, and searching for meaning in Eastern religions and Native American spirituality. "There was always a dissatisfaction, unease, questions," she says. "A lot of times I'd push it away, stuff it, and just go about the business of having a great life."

A registered nurse, Sue was the head of an open-heart, intensive-care unit at a prominent Cincinnati hospital. Her life was comfortable, with lots of possessions and lots of friends. She had gone back to school to complete her degree and was doing research at the public library downtown. "I started to notice homeless men and women coming in to get out of the cold," she recalls. "I began to see them outside, rooting through garbage cans for something to eat. I was startled." As comfortable as she was, Sue knew she had to do something. "I could not *not* respond. I felt a spark."

That spark led Sue to Bethany House Services (BHS), a shelter for homeless women and children in Cincinnati, where she began volunteering. Before long she found herself telling Sister Mary Stanton, BHS Director, about her struggles with the Catholic Church. Sister Mary, a Sister of Mercy, invited Sue to come and share prayer with her community. "I had an idea this would be Jesus and Hail Mary stuff," she laughs, "so I told her, 'No thanks.'" Later she was at Sister Mary's house for supper, and as Sue was leaving, Sister Mary again invited her to stay for prayer. "I did, and the prayer was beautiful, so universal, so accepting – wonderful."

During prayer, Sue shared how she had been feeling lost and estranged from the Catholic Church's theology and doctrine. "The feminine spirituality that the sisters were living opened the door to me. I learned about the liberation theology movement in Central America." Sue describes that evening as a conversion experience. "I was knocked right off my horse."

After working with homeless women at Bethany House Services, Sue saw a pattern. Families were homeless for the second and third time. She searched for a way to use her skills as a nurse to break the cycle. She found herself devoting all of her energy and thought to this. At the same time, she had volunteered to do home visits to the elderly for two Sisters of Mercy – Sister Mary Ann Fuerst and Sister Alice Marie Soete – who had a long-established ministry, the H.O.M.E. Program (House of Mercy Environment), serving elderly poor people in a Cincinnati neighborhood. During her home visits, Sue saw that these elderly poor needed more – a home care aide to help them with cooking, cleaning, and companionship.

"I was praying about all this," Sue recalls, "and I was reading about Catherine McAuley, foundress of the Sisters of Mercy, and the idea came in the middle of a restless sleep. Homeless women need education and employment to move beyond welfare, and the elderly need a home-care aide. I could teach the homeless women the skills to become home care aides."

This, she figured, would serve two needs, giving the homeless women meaningful skills and employment, while connecting them to the fragile elderly population.

"I was a critical care nurse," she explains, "I didn't know anything about community nursing. I didn't know anything about training or setting up a program," she laughs, "but I was on fire." She asked Sister Mary Stanton if Bethany House Services would sponsor the training. Then she called on a nurse friend who was running a home care agency for assistance.

Sister Alice Marie and Sister Mary Ann, excited at the prospect of help for their elderly, connected Sue with Kathy Durkee, a nurse and Mercy associate. Both Sue and Kathy agreed to be trained as instructors, developed a curriculum and got it approved by the Department of Health. Within nine months they had recruited their first class, taught it, graduated four women and hired them as their first employees.

Sue chose the name Healing Connections Associates (HCA) for the new organization. "Did we know what we were doing? No! It truly was an act of faith," she says. This seems to be the norm for HCA. "Every time I needed something," says Sue, "I was led to the person who could help. I believed that as long as we were open to the grace to recognize, everything we'd need would be given."

Sue describes this time as the fast track of her Mercy journey. She wanted to know everything about the foundress of the Sisters of Mercy. "The very first time I read Catherine McAuley's story I felt like she was my sister. It was as if I had always known her. I knew that her story was my story, but I didn't know what that meant. The work she had done with homeless women and children in the 1800s in Ireland – empowering poor women by providing education and jobs and self-sufficiency, bringing health care into the homes of the poor – this was the same work I was feeling called to do. The link was apparent. I recognized that in Mercy I had come home."

Taking on the founding and running of a not-for-profit agency was a giant leap for this attractive young woman. Accustomed to a level of comfort and independence as a single professional, Sue realized leaving her position as director of a nursing unit would require a dramatic change in lifestyle. She talked with Sister Mary about how she could simplify her life, and Sister Mary proposed she consider moving in with her and another sister and living in community. "I owned a house full of furniture," says Sue, "and I would have to do considerable downsizing. I wasn't sure how I'd be in community, but I was willing to try it."

This happened gradually, with Sue and Sister Mary exploring the idea. A lay woman living in community with sisters, without the intention of becoming a sister herself, had never been done before – at least not by the Sisters of Mercy. Some sisters in the community had reservations, but in the end, it became clear to all that Sue had a unique calling as a lay woman, and that living in community was appropriate. Sister Mary explained to Sue that if such a change felt wrenching or violent, then it wouldn't be from God. "I really took that to heart," Sue recalls. "This was a huge life change, but I never felt struggle or violence. It was a journey and it kept unfolding. So I sold all my possessions and moved into Mary's community. Talk about a conversion!"

Next, Sister Mary invited Sue to consider Mercy Association. "I thought and prayed about it. I sensed that this would be a life-changing commitment." In time Sue felt sure she had been given the charism and the call to make her covenant as a Mercy associate. Sue describes her experience as an associate as "becoming immersed in the Mercy community, putting my arms completely around the community and feeling the community put its arms completely around me. Over the course of time, the Mercy community of sisters and associates became more my family than my biological family."

Sue and Sister Mary still live together in a small frame house on the campus of Mother of Mercy High School in Cincinnati. Both Bethany House Services and Healing Connections Associates have grown during the years since the two women began the partnership in ministry and community life. They continue to support one another as they walk with homeless women and children who come to Bethany House Services, and they work to connect these women to the elderly served by the H.O.M.E. Program.

As each ministry has expanded, Sue and Sister Mary have had to deal with challenges. Valuable employees have left, yet new people appeared to fill the gap. Funding seemed to dry up, requiring cutbacks and strenuous fundraising projects, but eventually funds began to pour in again. Sister Mary was diagnosed with breast cancer and her treatment required considerable energy from both women. Together they have been able to celebrate Sister Mary's full recovery.

Sue refers to a "dry time," a few years ago, when she got so busy with her work at HCA that she was rushing through prayer, not paying attention. Part of the Mercy spirit, she says, is to live a life of balance between contemplation and action. "I had slipped into a mode of thinking my job was about me. God was in it, but God had gotten pretty small." For God to take hold, Sue recalls, she had to enter the desert. Several people on her staff had resigned for various reasons, leaving her feeling depleted and empty. She had trouble sleeping. "How could I take over the whole program: all the clients, all the aides, all the fundraising? I was already stretched so far and so thin. I went into a place that was dark and full of despair. I felt abandoned."

It was her bond with the Mercy community, Sue says, that supported her during this dry time. Exhausted, she was finally able to sleep and felt a powerful revelation and reconnection with God, an overwhelming feeling of love, of peace. When she awoke, she felt no fear. She spent most of the day in prayer, feeling energy and an overwhelming peacefulness. "I remembered how, every time I had felt at a loss on this journey, I had received the grace I needed. I was ready to trust God again that everything we'd need would be given."

A plan emerged to reorganize Healing Connections Associates in a way that has made it and everyone connected to it stronger. "This journey as a Mercy associate has been so incredibly enriching," says Sue, "and the joy has been intense."

Sue has a vision for religious orders, and for the Sisters of Mercy of the Americas in particular. She sees membership in religious orders expanding, beyond the forms we know now. She believes she is called to be part of that process. "I believe it is coming because it's the work of the Spirit. There's wonderful wisdom in the Mercy sisters and associates. I believe we'll be able to be co-creators of whatever shape religious orders may take in the future."

Sue believes there are other men and women like her who feel called to something that's between what we know now as association and vowed membership. "We haven't defined it," she says. "I'm just living it and so are other men and women. I identify with association but I also identify with the sisters. It's almost as if I'm a bridge between them."

Many of the sisters, even Sue's own mother, ask her why she doesn't just join the Mercy order. She says it's not what she's been called to do. "It's not that I don't ask the question or take it to prayer. But what I've come to realize is that I can't shape the future from inside the community. I have to help be a co-creator, from the outside, of what's coming." She explains that for now, association is what's available. She admits she's different from a lot of associates, in terms of the depth and breadth of her commitment and involvement.

For now, Sue is content to live *into* the new reality – that middle ground between life as a layperson and life as a vowed member in community. In her view, community is a much bigger concept than just the people one lives with. "Living with a group of people isn't my goal. It's being actively *immersed* in community, sharing our responsibilities and our resources." This includes financial resources, she adds.

Sue looks back over the years since that day in the public library when she became aware of homeless men and women and felt the spark. She's been knocked from her proverbial horse again and again. "Association with Mercy," she says, "has kept me on the right path. Even on the darkest, driest days, I know I can keep going."

Thirteen

Mary Jo Borgman Mersmann

Associate of the Sisters of Charity

Now there are varieties of gifts, but the same Spirit; and there are varieties of services, but the same God.. . for in one Spirit we were all baptized into one body... not of one member but of many.   *1 Corinthians 12:4-5, 13-14*

*M*ary Jo Mersmann looks across the grounds of the Motherhouse of the Sisters of Charity of Cincinnati, the well-tended lawns, the shaded cemetery where, since the early nineteenth century, sisters have been laid to rest. She brushes past the construction dust toward her office in the sprawling red-brick building now under renovation, as the sisters prepare for the future. As Director of Associates in Mission with the Sisters of Charity, Mary Jo sees this Motherhouse, this place, as her second home.

From first grade through senior year, Mary Jo felt close to her teachers, many of whom were Sisters of Charity. Still, when she graduated from Seton High School in 1967, and one of her friends announced she was entering the convent to become a Sister of Charity, Mary Jo did not feel the same call. Her girlfriend, Joyce, went her separate way, and for some years both were unaware how the sisters would bring them together again.

Mary Jo attended college but left after two years. She got a job, married, and was a stay-at-home mom for her three children, until her youngest, a son, entered kindergarten. "I was looking for something more," she recalls, "and since I had volunteered at my parish, the associate pastor suggested I look into the local Lay Pastoral Ministry Program." She did, graduating with a certificate in pastoral ministry in 1988. Soon after, she began working at the parish, Our Lady of Victory, located just a few miles from Mount St. Joseph, a college staffed by the Sisters of Charity. Since many of the sisters attended her parish, Mary Jo had the opportunity to reconnect with them.

She also reconnected with her friend, Joyce. "After she entered the convent, we lost touch for a while," says Mary Jo, "but eventually we started writing to one another and visiting when she was in town. We led very different lives, but we did keep in touch."

When it came time for Mary Jo's two daughters to attend high school, there was no question, she says, that they would be educated at her alma mater. Both daughters went on to college at Mount St. Joseph. "I suppose you could say our family became ingrained with the spirit and mission of the Sisters of Charity," she says.

While working at her parish, Mary Jo pursued her undergraduate degree. "Mount St. Joseph allowed me to apply some of my credits from the pastoral ministry program to a religious studies major," she says. On weekends, evenings and during the summer, Mary Jo attended classes, where she met other Sisters of Charity who were either teaching or attending classes with her. The sisters recognized her leadership, her drive and dedication to her faith. "They were my cheerleaders," she says, "and they encouraged me to keep going." She graduated *summa cum laude* in 1997 as a non-traditional student, the same day her oldest daughter graduated with her elementary education degree, *summa cum laude*, as a traditional student. Mother and daughter had been honored with the college's two highest awards. "It was such a joy for us to share this moment." Then Mary Jo laughs, "Of course, it took me thirty years after high school to get my degree, and my daughter Karen did it in four!"

What is it that drew this single mother to become an associate in mission with the Sisters of Charity? "I'm not a joiner," she says, "so when the first invitation came in the early 1990s, I wasn't too interested. I went to a few meetings, but it didn't fit for me at the time." Again in 1999, another invitation came by way of the director, Sister Mary Ann Humbert, who was forming small groups to share their faith experience. "This appealed to me, so I kept coming," she says. By the following year, Mary Jo felt ready to begin the process of making a full commitment to association. She attended orientation sessions, joined in worship and community celebrations with the sisters and other associates, and continued to attend a faith-sharing group. At the end of one year, in 2001, she was ready to commit as an associate.

One year later, when Sister Mary Ann announced she was stepping down from her position as director, a strange thing happened. Mary Jo received letters, emails, and phone calls. They all had the same basic message: "We hope you'll apply for the position."

"It was as if the Spirit were speaking to me," she recalls. "Such an affirmation. I prayed about it and talked it over with my family and friends. It felt so right." After a series of interviews and a period of discernment, both she and the community believed the time was right for a lay associate director, and agreed Mary Jo was the person for the job.

Of course, there were reservations. The first and most obvious was that she was not a Sister of Charity, and had only been an associate for one year. The community had had associates since 1973, but the director had always been a religious sister.

Some knew that she had recently been through a divorce and may have wondered how a divorced mother of three would fit as the director of people associated in mission with vowed religious women. However, when it was announced that Mary Jo would be the new director, the response was overwhelmingly positive. "I received support from sisters and associates, not just here at the Motherhouse," she says, "but from all over the country."

In her role as Director of Associates, Mary Jo sees this time as "exciting and frightening." The fear, she explains, arises from the realities of an aging community, with fewer and fewer young women choosing the vowed life. But Mary Jo's eyes light up as she describes the excitement she feels looking toward the future. "These sisters are courageous women," she says. "It's because of their vision thirty years ago to include the laity in their mission," says Mary Jo, "and their willingness to allow us to share in their spirit, that our associate program is so strong and vibrant today. They deserve the credit."

It's also exciting to Mary Jo that she and other associates have been charged with continuing the charism of the Sisters of Charity, based on their foundress, Elizabeth Bayley Seton, the first native-born American saint. Mother Seton, as she is known, was a mother with five children. Not that Mary Jo is aspiring to sainthood - or to life in a convent. "My kids had suspicions that, because I was spending so much time with the sisters, eventually I would become one." Mary Jo dispelled those suspicions when she announced that she and long-time friend Barry Mersmann, a widower, had decided to get married. At their wedding, the sisters joined in the celebration. "They've become my extended family."

Mary Jo brings many gifts to her position as director of associates. "I'm a real person, and I think that's what associates and sisters appreciate about me," Mary Jo says. "They've watched me recover from divorce, raise three kids, complete my degree, fall in love again. The associates know I can relate to their lives."

Mary Jo is an advocate for the 138 associates in mission across the country in twenty states, with more candidates in formation. "Sometimes the sisters are not accustomed to including associates in some aspects of community life. It isn't an intentional exclusion. I'm there to make sure associates are a part of the process, that we're not just an afterthought." She sees herself as a communicator and a bridge-builder, as she travels around the country to meet with associates or give presentations, educating sisters on the roles associates can play.

"Associates are in total support of the sisters' ministries," explains Mary Jo, "whether they actually work in those ministries or not." In the case of the Sisters of Charity, whose mission is education, social work, and health-related ministries, most associates have found their own ways of sharing the order's spirit. "Most of all," says Mary Jo, "people want to belong to something greater than themselves, and they don't always find this sense of belonging in a parish. Through association, we live out the mission of charity in our own lives, spiritually connected to the sisters."

As director, Mary Jo also sees herself as a future planner. "I'm always asking where we fit in, looking for a way to be part of the mission." Mary Jo's husband is involved in the training of men for service as deacons, and she can see similarities. "Deacons have a different call than priests," she says, "but both are valid calls, and they work closely together. The same is true for sisters and associates."

However, for Mary Jo, the fact that associates are not legally bound by the canon laws of the Roman Catholic Church, which apply to most religious orders, is an important distinction. "We are led by the Spirit, but we are not bound by canon law," she says, "and it feels necessary to preserve that difference."

Mary Jo sees herself providing a balance between the structure of religious life and the flexibility of associate membership. "Association needs a definite form, but not too much. Not everyone is at the same place regarding how much structure should be imposed. We're living with a lot of questions. As long as we keep living and stay open, life will provide the answers."

What does it mean to be an associate in mission with the Sisters of Charity? Although sisters and associates are spread across the United States, groups of associates meet in regions monthly. Sisters join them to connect and support one another in their daily lives. Associates also attend regular assemblies, celebrations and community meetings convened by the sisters. Small groups of associates and sisters also meet to share their faith journey. A biweekly newsletter and group email messages are other ways to stay connected.

As the number of vowed religious diminishes, associate membership grows. Mary Jo speculates about what association will look like in five, ten, twenty years. "I don't see us taking over religious orders," she says, "that's not our calling. But I do see associates as an important part of the future of religious orders. We are certainly one of the ways the spirit of the order, the charism of the founder, will continue to be lived out."

Mary Jo says her husband has not yet expressed an interest in being an associate. "He's more familiar with a hierarchical world, so I've been educating him in the ways of feminine spirituality," she says. "He attends worship celebrations with me here at the Motherhouse and enjoys being here. The sisters have made him feel so welcome. So, we'll see. Association is an individual calling." Mary Jo adds that she's thrilled to see more men choosing to become associates.

And what has become of her childhood friend, Joyce, who became a Sister of Charity right out of high school? Mary Jo smiles. "She's right here at the Motherhouse, so we see one another all the time." Are they still friends? "The best," Mary Jo says. "She's my encouragement. She has been a huge support to me and the associate program for many years."

More and more, sisters are welcoming lay men and women as associates, notes Mary Jo. "The lay person is capable. All of us received the same call at Baptism. That's why association is so attractive to lay people. That's why it's important for religious orders to welcome associates." Mary Jo states emphatically that this view into the future is not depressing. "It's exciting, refreshing. In five years, our associates will feel even more empowered to be Charity to the world!"

God Loves Stories

A Reflection for Individuals and Groups

If you are at this place in the book, then you have just finished reading stories of folks like you, men and women who have responded to God's invitation in their lives. And it has taken them on a marvelous journey. The roads may not have led far from home. Our most important journeys usually don't. The journey we are on is the inner journey, the soul journey, where we meet the God who dwells within, and our lives are never the same after that.

Everyone has a story. Maybe it is time to tell yours. What are you waiting for? Let this be an invitation to you to explore your own story, your own faith journey. Let's start with prayer. Create a prayerful setting for yourself. You may want to invite some companions along with you on this journey. Light a candle. Open the Scripture. Ask God to sit with you as you pray.

Song: Listen to, or sing one of the following:
The Summons, by Iona Community
For the Life of the World, by David Haas
God Has Chosen Me, by Bernadette Farrell

Prayer: My God, I have no idea where I am going,
I do not see the road ahead of me,
I cannot know for certain where it will end.
Nor do I really know myself,
and the fact that I think that I am following your will
does not mean that I am actually doing so.
But I believe that the desire to please you
    does in fact please you.
And I hope I have that desire in all that I am doing.
And I know that if I do this,
you will lead me on the right road.

Thomas Merton

Story:

When the great Rabbi Israel Baal Shem Tov saw misfortune threatening the Jews it was his custom to go into a certain part of the forest to meditate. There he would light a fire, say a special prayer, and the miracle would be accomplished and the misfortune averted. Later, when his disciple, the celebrated Magid of Mezritch, had occasion, for the same reason, to intercede with heaven, he would go to the same place in the forest and say: "Master of the Universe, listen! I do not know how to light the fire, but I am still able to say the prayer." Again the miracle would be accomplished.

Still later, Rabbi Moshe-leib of Sasov, in order to save his people once more, would go into the forest and say: "I do not know how to light the fire. I do not know the prayer; but I know the place and this must be sufficient." It was sufficient and the miracle was accomplished. Then it fell to Rabbi Israel of Rizhyn to overcome misfortune. Sitting in his armchair, his head in his hands, he spoke to God: "I am unable to light the fire, and I do not know the prayer; I cannot even find the place in the forest. All I can do is to tell the story, and this must be sufficient." And it was sufficient. God made man [humanity] because God loves stories.

Elie Weisel, *The Gates of the Forest*

Reflection Questions: What is my story?

Scripture:

I know well the plans I have in mind for you, says the Lord, plans for your welfare and not for woe! Plans to give you a future full of hope. When you call me, when you go to pray to me, I will listen to you. When you look for me, you will find me. Yes, when you seek me with all your heart, you will find me with you, says the Lord, and I will change your lot.

Jeremiah 29:11-14

Reading:

Today I understand vocation quite differently - not as a goal to be achieved but as a gift to be received. Discovering vocation does not mean scrambling toward some prize just beyond my reach but accepting the treasure of true self I already possess. Vocation does not come from a voice "out there" calling me to become something I am not. It comes from a voice "in here" calling me to be the person I was born to be, to fulfill the original selfhood given me at birth by God. Our deepest calling is to grow into our own authentic selfhood, whether or not it conforms to some image of who we ought to be. As we do so, we will not only find the joy that every human being seeks—we will also find our path of authentic service in the world. True vocation joins self and service, as Frederick Buechner asserts when he defines vocation as "the place where your deep gladness meets the world's deep need."

Let Your Life Speak, by Parker Palmer

Reflection Questions:

So many times we think of a call, or vocation, only in terms of being a priest, or a member of a religious congregation. We often forget the initial call we received was at Baptism, the call to holiness.

How do I live out my baptismal call?

What is God calling me to at this time in my life?

Would connecting my life with the life of a religious community as an associate, companion, or partner help me live out God's call?

Closing Prayer:

> Holy One of Blessing,
> Giver of all life and beauty,
> You love us into being.
> We stand before you in gratitude for calling us,
> alone and together, into our journey of life.
> Bless us with the grace to recognize your gifts
>   when they are given,
> to own them, to claim them,
> to acknowledge them as ours to give away.
> Amen.

We have one solid comfort amidst this tripping about, that our hearts are always in the same place, centered in God, for whom alone we go forward or stay back.

Catherine McAuley, founder of the Sisters of Mercy

Wanda Smith, RSM

Appendix A

Highlights from
*Partners in Mission: A Profile of Associates and
Religious in the United States*
NACAR Study 2000

The North American Conference of Associates and Religious (NACAR), working with the Center for Applied Research in the Apostolate (CARA), completed a groundbreaking survey in the spring of 2000 entitled, *Partners in Mission: A Profile of Associates and Religious in the United States.*

Although the dream of such a study lived in the minds and hearts of many, it was not until the 1998 publication of the Canadian Associate Survey that the first concrete steps were taken to bring life to that dream. The survey's questionnaire was completed in the fall of 1999 and was sent to over 11,000 religious congregations across the United States. With a return rate of 75%, the survey identified a total of 27,400 associates across the United States with another 2,700 in formation. Statistical data collected reveals the exciting story of a revolutionary movement in the Church. These numbers reflect an increase of over 10,000 from the number identified by a survey completed by Hembrecht and Rose in 1995. Unlike the Hembrecht/Rose survey, the NACAR study surveyed both male and female congregations and in its report broke down the data in several areas by gender.

Associate is the term used by 76% of the responding institutes to designate those lay men and women who chose to enter into a formal relationship with the institute. Using the working definition of *associate* as *a defined way which those outside vowed membership can share in the mission and goals of a religious institute,* 52% of the respondents stated they indeed have associates, while 5% planned to begin associations in the future. Institutes of women religious are more likely than institutes of male religious to have associates, and they are also more likely to have had associations for a longer period of time.

What does the face of an associate look like? The data reveals that in the United States, associates are more likely to be female (19,665 or 84% compared to 3,789 men or 16% of the total), revealing that women outnumber their male counterparts by five to one. An associate is more likely to be a lay person and married (63%), next, lay and single (33%), then, either a religious or diocesan priest or permanent deacon (4%).

Although associates of both genders are highly concentrated in the upper age brackets, particularly in the range of 50 to 69, there are significant numbers of associates in the 30 to 50 age group; the median age of associates is about ten years younger than their religious counterparts.

The vast majority of associates are Caucasian (88% in female communities compared to 70% in male communities). However, other racial and ethnic groups are represented, particularly in male communities where associates with African American, Asian, or Pacific Island backgrounds comprise almost 30% of the total number, compared to 13% for women's communities.

The survey also shows continued growth in the story of associates. With the number of associate candidates in formation or orientation currently at 2,692 (2,246 women and 446 men), it is obvious that the Holy Spirit has not finished writing the story.

Jean Sonnenberg, ACBS
Co-Founder, NACAR

Appendix B
Web sites of Religious Communities

Chapter One
Mary O'Connor
Sisters of Mercy of the Americas
Regional Community of Dallas
www.somdallasreg.org

Chapter Two
Hans Hallundbaek
Maryknoll Missioners
www.maryknoll.org

Chapter Three
Martina Kocher
Dominican Sisters of Springfield, IL
www.springfieldop.org

Chapter Four
Isabel G. Tobey
Congregation of Incarnate Word and Blessed Sacrament
www.incarnatewordorder.org

Chapter Five
Dee Nelson
Dominican Sisters of Springfield, IL
www.springfieldop.org

Chapter Six
Don and Mary Kreilkamp
Missionaries of the Precious Blood
www.cpps-preciousblood.org

Chapter Seven
Audrey Bagnowski
Sisters of St. Francis, Sylvania, OH
www.sistersosf.org

Chapter Eight
Guy Mazzola
Congregation of Incarnate Word and Blessed Sacrament
www.incarnatewordorder.org

Chapter Nine
Elizabeth Browne
Partner of the Passionist Fathers
www.passionist.org

Chapter Ten
Terry Ulery
Missionaries of the Precious Blood
www.cpps-preciousblood.org

Chapter Eleven
Tim Simmons
Sisters of Mercy of the Americas
Regional Community of Merion
www.sistersofmercymerion.org

Chapter Twelve
Suzanne Kathman
Sisters of Mercy of the Americas
Regional Community of Cincinnati
www.mercycincinnati.org

Chapter Thirteen
Mary Jo Borgman Mersmann
Sisters of Charity of Cincinnati
www.srcharitycinti.org

Author

Kathleen Wade, Mercy Associate

A writer and teacher of writing in Cincinnati, Kathy has had her poetry and essays published in a variety of anthologies and periodicals. This is her first full-length work. Kathy is Assistant Director and a teacher at Women Writing for (a) Change, a feminist writing school for women and girls in Cincinnati. She was educated by Sisters of Mercy and was a member of the religious order from 1960 to 1972. Since 1999 she has been Regional Coordinator of Mercy Volunteer Corps for the Sisters of Mercy, Regional Community of Cincinnati. Kathy and her husband, Forrest Brandt, also a writer, have been Mercy associates since 1996.

Collaborators

Carren Herring, R.S.M.

Sister Carren Herring has been a Sister of Mercy since 1959. She has been an elementary school teacher and principal in Catholic schools in Ohio and in Jamaica, West Indies. Currently she is Director of the Eastern Catholic Alliance of Schools for Excellence (E-CASE), a consortium of nine schools who work together for excellence. Sister Carren is also Co-Director of Mercy Association for the Sisters of Mercy, Regional Community of Cincinnati.

Gertrude Stefanko

After teaching mathematics and art in Catholic schools for thirty-eight years, Gert Stefanko started a new career in graphic design in 1999. A Mercy associate with the Regional Community of Cincinnati since 1984, Gert finds much good work designing logos, newsletters, and brochures. She is also an accomplished silversmith and woodworker. Her creative handiwork has benefited non-profit organizations both in and outside the Mercy community.

Wanda Smith, R.S.M.

Sister Wanda Smith has been a Sister of Mercy since 1979. She has an M.A. in theology from Xavier University in Cincinnati, OH. Her ministry has included being a Pastoral Associate, Vocation Director, Associate Director and a member of the leadership team for the Sisters of Mercy, Regional Community of Cincinnati. Currently she spends her time in spiritual direction and retreat work.